WordSpeak

WordSpeak
His Word, Your Voice

Laura C. Bower

WinePressPublishing
Your Book, Defined.

ISBN 13: 978-1-60615-046-7
ISBN 10: 1-60615-046-4
Library of Congress Catalog Card Number: 2009909064

This book is dedicated to all those who walked this journey with me. To my kids, John, Mark, Jennie, and Gracie, who each in their own way pushed, prodded, challenged, and encouraged me. To my husband, Stan, my constant north star, for all the notes and flowers of encouragement. To the "Underground Sisterhood"—Carol Gunn and Pat Perry who prayed me through the tough places. To my "WordSpeak Prayer Square"—Jackie Nace, Marlene Johnson, Jennie Bower—who let me experiment with them. To my friends Beth Hullett and Mary Ellen Buchanan who laughed with me through it. To my trusted counselor, Dr. David Knight, who taught me how to care for myself. And finally, to my father, Lester B. Collins, on whose shoulders I stand.

Contents

Section One

On Your Mark!

Acknowledging God's Will

Trust in the Lord with all your heart, and lean not on your own understanding, In all your ways acknowledge Him, and He will make your path straight.

—Proverbs 3:5–6

Introduction

The effective prayer of a righteous man can accomplish much.

—James 5:16

Years ago, I stumbled upon a powerful principle of prayer that revolutionized my life. As a wife and mother of four children, I realized how powerless I was to control the people and circumstances swirling around me. Once I came to the end of my efforts and faced my helplessness to influence and protect those I truly cared for, I turned to God for help. I simply said, "There has to be more to this business of prayer. Teach me to pray."

With that brief, heartfelt prayer, the Lord enrolled me in my own personal "prayer school" where He began to expose me to the principles in the Scriptures of effective praying. As I practiced these principles I began to see amazing results. The more answers I experienced, the more I saw other principles embedded in the Word of God.

This newfound lifestyle of prayer birthed a revolutionary tool I have chosen to call WordSpeak®, which is a focused way to pray about the concerns of life. The information found in this book plus the accompanying Scripture Prayer Cards will guide you into a more powerful way to pray. The journey chronicled in this book is a story of transformation. After a long and adventurous journey, I present this prayer tool to help those who want to influence their world.

Sadly, most of us go through life without understanding the power of prayer. I discovered that communing with God, taking His words to heart, and declaring them over my circumstances greatly enhanced the effectiveness of my prayers. I learned how to look for and rely on His words in Scripture to influence how I prayed. Eventually, I learned an important lesson. As long as the words of God remain on the dusty pages of a Bible, they are only literature, but once given a voice they become living and active.

God's Word has enormous power. Throughout the ages the focus of prayer may have changed, but the wisdom of God's Word has not. Spiritual laws are written down in the Scriptures and cannot be revoked. Just as the laws of nature prevail in spite of our ignorance, so do spiritual laws. Knowledge of these laws enhances our lives. The precepts, principles, and promises of the Bible are guides to help us not only manage life, but also bring into order the unmanageable aspects of our life. Our effectiveness to bring divine order into our life flows out of an understanding of spiritual laws, and an accurate handling of the word of truth (2 Tim. 2:15).

Whenever God opened His mouth and spoke, things happened. The world was created and science was installed. God's Word is as powerful today as when first spoken. The inspired Word of God brings healing and restoration when given a voice. The ancient words of the Bible can influence current affairs when they are understood, believed, incorporated into one's life, and then given a voice. What we speak is imperfect, but when we genuinely couple our voice with the words of Scripture, we produce a powerful message.

There is power in purposeful, focused prayer—power to heal the consequences of the past, impact present circumstances, and shape future events. When present circumstances do not line up with a promise from the Word of God, you pray. When you need the Holy Spirit to shape future events or character, you pray. When sins or events committed in the past have negative consequences, you pray.

The sections *On Your Mark!, Get Set!,* and *Go!* will lead you to a successful WordSpeak journey. The book is laced with little *Lessons* that I learned along the way. They are actually foundational truths on which to build a solid life. Don't rush past them just because they are small. Bricks are also little, but they can build a mighty strong house. The *Power Principles* at the end of each short chapter provide the mortar.

The WordSpeak Prayer Cards are prayers based on scriptures that reflect God's heart on specific matters, conveniently categorized for easy access. With the aid of the prayer cards, I am reminded to pray throughout the day over whatever concern I might have. Posted in conspicuous places around my home and office, these scripture prayer cards became a lifeline to me—little reminders of God's truths. I also found them to be faith boosters and cue cards to speak over my stubborn problems. You can find the information on obtaining these WordSpeak products in the back of the book.

The purpose of this book is to help your voice be heard in the heavenly courts. The Bible says that if we ask anything according to the will of God, He hears us. Your voice and His Word is a powerful combination, bringing God's Word to bear on your circumstances. I pray that this book will help you make the divine connection and assist you as you live life in collaboration with His will and purposes. Your life will become a great adventure, I promise.

If we ask anything according to His will, He hears us.
And if we know that He hears us in whatever we ask
we know that we have the requests which we have asked from Him.

—1 John 5:14b–15

Chapter 1

The Prayer That Revolutionized

So shall My word be which goes forth from My mouth; it shall not return to Me empty, without accomplishing what I desire, and without succeeding in the matter for which I sent it.

—Isaiah 55:11

Anyone with a sick child understands the helpless feeling that comes with watching that child suffer. I watched my second son, Mark, suffer physically in the first years of his life. Born with a congenital heart problem, he was frail and prone to high fevers. It seemed he was always sick. This affected his attitude toward himself. His older brother, John, was robust and athletic, and I was concerned about comparison between them as Mark entered adolescence. One day as I read the Bible, this verse about Jesus' childhood struck me. "And he grew in wisdom and stature and in favor with God and men" (Luke 2:52).

Hmmm, I thought somewhat jealously. *I want my son to grow in wisdom and stature and in favor with God and with men.* So I began praying this verse word for word for my young son. I also declared it over him. "You are growing in wisdom and stature and in favor with God and men." Hearing myself say this over time, I prayed with more and more confidence and my faith increased.

Hmmm, I thought somewhat jealously. *I want my son to grow in wisdom and stature and in favor with God and with men.*

One evening at a neighborhood swim meet, Mark moved up in the ranks from his usual last place to first in all of his events. When he came out of the water, lean and taut, a father marched up to him, pulled him out of the water, and said, "Son, you are a fine specimen and a great swimmer. How is it I haven't seen you around my house? You should come over and meet my daughter." Of course, my heart burst with pride.

Not long after, Mark gave a testimony at a youth camp reflection service. Afterward, another father introduced himself, saying, "Son, let me shake your hand. Where have boys like you been? I'd like for you to come around and meet my daughters. Take your pick because you are welcome to date either of them."

I began to put two and two together and immediately went back to the Lord with some concern. "Okay, Lord, thank You for Your favor and the growth in my son, but maybe we should lay off the 'favor with man' part for a while—after all, he is only thirteen!"

You may chuckle and chalk it up to coincidence, but this prayer continued to be answered in Mark's life. At seventeen he was chosen to serve on a leadership team with other adults from the community. His older brother (a wise young man himself) said to me about his kid brother, "Mom, he is so wise!" Now how many college-aged kids would admit that about his sibling?

Without a doubt, my son did grow in wisdom and stature and in favor with God and man. Looking back, I marvel at the many doors of opportunity that opened to him specifically because of this wisdom and favor. Today Mark is a healthy, hearty, and rather stout young adult. All I did was pray God's Word over my child and watch His Word go to work, because "All Scripture is inspired by God and profitable . . . that the man of God may be adequate, equipped for every good work" (2 Tim. 3:16).

The Lesson:

God's Word is not confined to a particular time or place. Under the supervision of the Holy Spirit, it becomes living and active in any time and any place. "For the word of God is living and active . . ." (Heb. 4:12).

Power Principle:

The basics principles that I call the ABCs of WordSpeak, took many years to test and prove. Through many circumstances I discovered the most effective praying comes when I:

Ask for God's help and favor.
Believe God's Word is true and will come to pass.
Confess with my mouth the truth found in God's Word.

"Easier said than done," you may say. True. Though it might not be easy to know God's will in all the circumstances of our lives, it is not impossible. God wants to reveal His will to us through a process that involves some time and effort on our part. The foundation of a WordSpeak Journey is based on an amazing promise found in Luke 11:9–10:

Ask, and it shall be given to you;
Seek, and you shall find;
Knock, and it shall be opened to you.

I call this the ASK process. Simply put, when you pray, you ask God to meet a need. You seek by searching the Scriptures to find His will for your particular need. As you seek His will in His Word, you get your map and marching orders, so to speak, to know how to proceed in the prayer process. The WordSpeak Scripture cards are collected and categorized by topics to help you understand God's heart on a specific matter. Once this information is obtained you proceed to the knocking stage. At this point, knowing the will of God concerning your particular circumstances can mean the difference between bloody knuckles and an opened door.

WordSpeak is an effective tool for the knocking stage of the prayer process because the Scripture cards keep His words in your line of vision and can be easily accessed for praying aloud. Knocking is simply faith in action. Once you know God's will concerning a subject, and you believe in your heart that what God says in His Word is true, you can begin to speak His Word over your circumstance.

> When we knock we are saying, "Open up! Let God's will come through!"

When we knock we are saying, "Open up! Let God's will come through!" For too many years I mistakenly thought that knocking was trying to get through to God so He would hear me and let me in, a lie that kept me frustrated and ineffective in my prayer life. He is all too willing to hear us any time we call on Him.

In my journey, I discovered that knowing God's will and growing in faith are both tied to knowing God's Word. Because so many promises found in the Bible were news to me, I struggled to acquire a new mind-set. Could the promises of the Bible be applied to my problems? Could they come true for me? There was only one way to find out, "Be transformed by the renewing of your mind. Then you will be able to test and approve what God's will is—his good, pleasing and perfect will" (Rom. 12:2 NIV).

Although I didn't understand all the repercussions of what I had experienced that summer, I could hardly wait to find another such "word from the Lord" to use in my prayer life. I also did not realize that God was drawing me into a lifestyle of prayer that would not only affect my life but would also equip me to influence the world around me. In fact, my personal school of prayer had begun many years before. I just didn't know it . . .

Chapter 2

Accepting God's Will

*But the vessel that he was making of clay was spoiled in the hands
of the potter; so he remade it into another vessel, as it pleased
the potter to make.*

—Jeremiah 18:4

At the time, sitting on the floor was the best I could do to keep up with
my three small children. I was trapped in the web of chronic illness
and had little energy to play. From that vantage point, my eyes fell on a bright
pink book about prayer on the bottom of my bookshelf. Despairing of ever
being able to participate in our women's ministry at church, the thought hit
me, *I guess I could pray.* Suddenly I imagined myself as the invalid shut-in who
lay in bed and prayed all day for missionaries. "How boring," I said aloud.
Then another thought hit me. *There has to be more to this business of prayer.* As
I breathed those fateful words, "Lord, teach me to pray," something stirred
within me.

My life has taken so many unexpected turns since that day, but in traveling
to unfamiliar places I have learned so much about my God and His plan
for my life that I am eager to share my findings with you. The principles I
share in this guidebook are proven and effective. Over time, people began to
come to me with their concerns and I gained a certain reputation for seeing
breakthroughs in prayer. But I know it is not because of anything I am or
have except a personal relationship with the King of the universe. I love Him
and He loves me, and I have learned how to collaborate with Him who holds
the universe in His hands. You can as well.

You do not need to be an "expert" in prayer. You do not have to rely on a priest or a minister. God is no respecter of persons. He loves to talk with His children and give them the desires of their hearts, and He is available twenty-four hours a day. The information found in this guidebook will help you along the journey of getting to know God, which is what prayer is all about—knowing Him and learning how to collaborate with Him in this adventure called life.

You might be surprised to see the metamorphosis of my life. Timidity and passivity defined my code of conduct and took a toll. For reasons I now understand better, I became afraid to make my own decisions for fear of "stepping outside of God's will."

God's will was a big deal to me as a youngster. I had listened to my father, a Southern Baptist preacher, deliver many an impassioned plea to follow God's plan. Overhearing the tragedies of so many of the lives my father and mother shepherded, I concluded their pain was due to stepping outside of God's will. Whatever God's will was, I certainly didn't want to be outside of it! If I had made any inner vows, this was one of them—never, ever to step outside the lines.

My father's success as a preacher caused him to be much sought after. But after attending three elementary schools, three junior high schools, and two high schools, I learned to take what I got. Being the preacher's kid had its advantages, but it set me apart, making it hard for me to make a friend. By the time I was in college a well-entrenched pattern existed. Totally unprepared for the multitude of choices thrown at me, I rarely made a move or a decision for myself. "*Que sera, sera*, whatever will be, will be" was my theme song. I was afraid to make mistakes so I simply let things happen—"*C'est la vie!*"

I wasn't even brave enough to choose my own roommates for fear of "stepping outside of God's will." I let life (confusing it with God) make choices for me, sometimes with disastrous results. My father recognized this dangerous abdication

"When are you going to quit being the victim and start being the victor?"

and, in his only handwritten letter to me in college, asked a question that startled me. "When are you going to quit being the victim and start being the victor?" I hardly knew what to make of it.

Unaware that I had made the choice to be a victim, I acquired a lot of experience in that role early in my young adulthood. If someone wanted to take me out on a date, I could not refuse even against my better judgment, a practice that put me in more than one dangerous situation. I spent a long, terrifying night in a park, trapped by a man who turned psychotic after drinking, still not understanding how I got there.

My lack of self-esteem took me down devastating pathways. One of the most demoralizing was allowing others to choose a man I married, resulting in a psychological oppression that left me broken deep inside. Subconsciously, I knew it was wrong, but I couldn't seem to stop the swell of activity that swept me down the aisle. My intuition that this was wrong turned out to be correct, and my life took a terrible turn for the worse. Mercifully, after a short process, I was handed some papers one day and told that I wasn't married anymore, along with the advice to "get out on the streets and get some experience." I didn't seek a divorce, nor did I employ a lawyer for representation. I simply took what I got. Though the experience was short-lived, its effects were long lasting.

I was imprisoned by a feeling that I could not ask anything for myself. A feeling of helplessness enveloped me. I felt that everything I did was wrong and happiness would evade me. Instead of learning to think for myself, I went underground. Unable to face my failure, I simply began to live as if none of it had ever happened and looked for someone else to take care of me. Denial is a dangerous state of being, but like many others, I embraced it as a friend.

> Denial is a dangerous state of being, but like many others, I embraced it as a friend.

Soon I met a strong Christian young man who would provide the shelter I needed as I began to emerge as a person and experience for the first time the full range of emotions. I jumped into marriage with my husband, Stan, before I discovered what was wrong with my approach to life. Subconsciously wanting to cover my shame, I entered into this most important union immature, undeveloped, and unprepared for the storms life would throw at us.

Stan came from an anger-based home, but neither my husband nor I understood the underlying anger that plagued our marriage. We were both Christians, wholeheartedly dedicated to the Lord and His service, but our emotions were a mess. I don't remember how long I fiercely clung to the role of the long-suffering Christian woman graciously accepting all ills without protest, but I remember the day my facade crumbled.

After ten years of one crisis after another, I crashed. Broken, with tears streaming down my face, I ran from my husband into my closet and, while pushing him away, screamed, "I'm tired of being the good little Christian girl. It doesn't work. Nothing goes right for us! I hate you! I want a divorce!" Sadly enough, that could have been my most authentic moment up to that point in my life. My sweet, demure demeanor had been all I had known to do, but life had pushed me to the limits.

Fortunately, my husband, Stan, was stalwart in the face of a crisis and stayed around to see the outcome. He understood the strain of the past years. He also took ownership of the toll his behavior had taken on our relationship. But neither of us understood how such a hardworking man as he could remain in a constant state of financial insufficiency. I didn't really want a divorce, I just wanted out of the constant pain. I felt like resigning from the Christian life. "Woe to the one who quarrels with his Maker . . ." Will the clay say to the potter, "What are you doing?" (Isa. 45:9).

> Had I lived a life of ease I would have remained a soft, weak Christian whose beliefs were only theory.

I know now that my brokenness was allowed by a very wise Potter, who had something better in mind for me than the shape my life had taken. Had I lived a life of ease I would have remained a soft, weak Christian whose beliefs were only theory. Some may have preferred the soft-spoken southern girl who saw life through the looking glass that "all things work together for good" as long as all things are easy and delightful. I could have remained in this childlike state, but God in His goodness chose otherwise for me. He allowed my life to be shattered in order for me to truly live.

For me to fulfill the purposes of my life, God had to remold and remake me. Removing my reliance on my own understanding was the only way for me to learn to trust Him with all my heart. He wanted to bring me out of that closet, so to speak, and use me to share with others the powerful principles I was learning in another type of closet—the prayer closet.

The Lesson:

In the hands of the Potter, a shattered life can lead us to our destiny. The circumstances of our lives mold us into vessels for God's own purposes. "For we are His workmanship, created in Christ Jesus for good works, which God prepared beforehand so that we would walk in them" (Eph. 2:10).

Power Principle:

If God has allowed the trials of life to shatter you, stop quarreling with Him and ask Him to bless His purposes for the pain. Hold on to the belief that God doesn't want you to remain crushed. In the midst of the trial, allow Him to comfort you. Cry out for His comfort, beg for His healing touch. Lessons will become clear much later. He wants to demolish the untruths of your life and bring you into His reality. You will be better off, I promise. By willfully placing yourself in His hands, you can relax, knowing there is purpose in the pain.

> If God has allowed the trials of life to shatter you, stop quarreling with Him and ask Him to bless His purposes for the pain.

The stories in this book paint a picture of a beautiful redemptive story—an angry dad transforming into a gentle giant and a meek mom becoming a fierce warrior. Through a lifetime of lessons, I learned that I must take up my life and live it consciously.

God taught me how to fight for my life in order to live victoriously, my textbook being the Bible, my tutor the Holy Spirit. I learned that good things don't always just happen. Sometimes we must stand against the enemy's plans and choose paths that lead to better outcomes. Before, I didn't think I had an enemy in the world. Now I know better.

> I have finally learned to disagree with the enemy's lesser plan and choose God's greater good *even when the evidence of it is nowhere in sight.*

Through these years I learned to recognized the tactics of Satan, who presents his dark suggestions in my mind cloaked in words of truth. In order to recognize his lies, I had to first know the truth as stated in the Word of God. I have finally learned to disagree with the enemy's lesser plan and choose God's greater good *even when the evidence of it is nowhere in sight.* The crises of life became my classroom for learning the most important lessons, some of which I will share with you. I hope to show you how I filled my life with the words of God and began to use them to sculpt my words and direct my prayers. Now I understand that we avoid trouble and walk in greater favor when we walk according to the spiritual laws of the kingdom of heaven.

The principles in the Scriptures became living, active guides that accompanied me throughout these storms and set my feet on solid ground. Filling my mind with God's words gave me the language of the Spirit, which He spoke to me and through me to bring down the barriers and bring in the abundance God planned for my life. I pray my journey will inspire you to do the same.

Chapter 3

The God Who Sees

She gave this name to the LORD who spoke to her: "You are the God who sees me," for she said, "I have now seen the One who sees me."

—Genesis 16:13 (NIV)

The black day in the closet when I uttered those terrible words about wanting to resign from the Christian life, my husband had just returned from selling some of his guns in order to buy gasoline to drive from Houston to Kerrville to attend Christian Businessmen's family camp. This was the straw that broke me, as I realized no matter how hard we tried, we always seemed to end up destitute. We desperately needed a little break. I had garage sales, worked odd jobs mowing lawns with the kids, taught piano lessons, scrimping for months to put aside a little money for a mini-vacation to go to Sea World the weekend after the camp.

The day before we were to leave, the radiator in the car blew, and we had to replace it, taking the total amount of money I had saved. Grappling with disappointment, I hid in the garage so the kids would not see my tears. Yet even in this I struggled to maintain a right attitude.

"Lord, I've worked so hard and saved so long for this little vacation. I don't understand. I guess I should be thankful that at least we had the money to pay for the radiator. But we so needed some fun."

I was able to gain my balance again, but just barely. We still had the family camp ahead of us but I wasn't looking forward to it. I was unfamiliar with the people and I wasn't in the mood for more Bible teaching. When I got the news that we couldn't even afford the gas to get there, my wheels came flying off! In my precarious emotional state, it was more than I could handle. I was sick and tired and at the point of despair, and couldn't seem to pull myself together. But we had been given a scholarship and could not back out now, no matter what state I was in.

My husband had never seen me fall completely apart like this. I was generally a go-along-to-get-along type of gal, but at that point I could hardly put one foot in front of another. I just couldn't put on my "everything's okay" face mask.

"Come on, Laura. It'll be fun," he urged. And then he said those magic words, "Hey, for five whole days you won't have to cook."

"Fine, but I'm not going to go to the meetings and listen to another preacher tell me God is in control," I said bitterly.

For years my husband told me God was stripping us to make us more dependent upon Him. But after so many years of God's "stripping" I wasn't getting better, I was getting bitter. Deep disappointment in God, my life, and my faith had taken its toll. I could no longer pretend to be the good, Christian girl I had always thought I was. I had been such a trooper for all these years, trying to live for God, speak for God, and witness for Him in the face of deep distresses. But deep inside I felt like my faith had betrayed me, and all I had trusted in washed away.

Moving along in a near catatonic state, I found myself in the car driving the five hours to our destination. Arriving at the camp just in time for dinner, we registered and lined up for the first meal. After getting our food and settling our kids, I began the duties of cutting the meat on my child's plate. Disconnected and dejected, I barely noticed those around me. I was on auto-pilot, just wanting to hide.

An elderly gentlemen and a young man sat down across the table in front of me. The older man introduced himself as Major Ian Thomas and his "mule," Jonathon. After a few more exchanges, it became apparent to me that this was, indeed, the Bible teacher for the week.

O, great, I thought, *just what I need, to try to make small talk with the main speaker.* I wanted to stay as far away as I could from anyone championing the Christian life. But my training took over and I managed to ask a polite question I truly wasn't interested in, "So, what do you do?"

In his jocular English accent, Major Thomas explained that he was "traipsing around the world delivering a message of hope to the poor, worn-out Christian who is at the point of despair." His brief, but pointed answer pierced my hard heart and tears of resignation sprung to my eyes. My face aflame, I turned to my attention to my child's plate and began cutting her meat—again, surprised to hear myself reply, "Well, I'm poor, and I'm tired, and I'm at the point of despair."

Completely nonplussed, Major Thomas answered in the kindest tone, "Well, good then, perhaps God has something to say to you this week."

A warmth spread over my face and spirit as I felt the walls around my heart begin to crumble. How we could have experienced such an intimate exchange in only moments was beyond me. I still felt certain I would not attend the Bible studies. As we left the dining hall to check into our rooms, I relaxed a bit, thinking I would skip the evening session and recuperate in my room.

Our accommodation was one of four rooms connected by a living area where the campers would spend many evening socializing and discussing the lessons of the week. Much to my dismay, Major Thomas brushed passed me with a cheery "Hello again" and continued on to his room right next door to us! A few minutes later he breezed past our open door just long enough to greet us and say, "Well then, see you there? Cheerio!"

Ugh. It was then I knew I wasn't going to get away with anything this week. I felt like the school kid trying to play hooky. Not that Major Thomas knew of my subversive plans, nor my struggle to even be there. God's Spirit was using him to gently herd me over to the meeting where a lifetime of misunderstanding would be swept away in favor of the real truths of how to live the Christian faith.

As it turned out, that camp and the encounters of the week would prove to be a turning point in our lives. With the inspired Bible teaching of Major Thomas and the marriage advice from David and Teresa Ferguson of Intimate Life Ministries, we were handed truths and tools that would last a lifetime. Unbeknown to me, many of these people had been praying for the two of us and were concerned about our welfare. I had the opportunity to ask questions of this most amazing Bible teacher, who kindly accepted my barely hidden bitterness without a hint of judgment. As the week went on it seemed there was an army of people who had been praying for us.

The last day of the camp one of the campers who had been praying for us leaned over the chair beside me and handed me a book, saying, "I thought of you when I read this." As I read Oswald Chamber's *My Utmost for His Highest*, I realized that none of these people knew the details of my struggle, and yet, God was using each of them to send me a personal message:

> Clouds are those sorrows or sufferings or providences, within or without our personal lives, which seem to dispute the rule of God. It is by those very clouds that the Spirit of God is teaching us how to walk by faith.

> The clouds are a sign that He is there . . . It is not true to say that God wants to teach us something in our trials: through

every cloud He brings, He wants us to unlearn something. His purpose in the cloud is to simplify our belief until our relationship to Him is exactly that of a child—God and my own soul.

Unless we can look the darkest, blackest fact full in the face without damaging God's character, we do not yet know Him.

That was the lesson of the week for me. I did not yet know God as He wanted to be known. These years of clouds were evidence that God was drawing near, not abandoning me. These trials were not haphazard nor arbitrary. I needed to unlearn some things. Sure, it was great to hear Major Thomas' message that in order to live the Christian life successfully, we must let Jesus live it through us, like a hand in a glove, we being the glove and Jesus the motivating force. Sure, it was good to learn how to live life more emotionally connected with our mates. But the

I was in God's sights. He saw me. He knew the state I was in, and He moved on my behalf.

greatest lesson for me was this: I was in God's sights. He saw me. He knew the state I was in, and He moved on my behalf. I heard Him loud and clear. I felt His touch and knew He cared about my brokenness.

My heart began to trust that He was not going to leave me alone in this fight of my life. He was going to fight with me and for me. He knew where I was, and He loved me enough to send His only Son, Jesus, to rescue me from darkness. Yes, I had heard that sermon many times before, but his time it was different. This time it was for me.

Jesus truly became my Messiah, a rescue for sinners, not just for eternity, but also for my life today. He rescued me through an opportunity to go to a Christian camp where we began relationships that would bring us a lifetime of support. Stan had simply believed God would take care of his broken little wife, and he acted on that belief by dragging me to my first family camp, even if he had to "hock" some guns to get us there.

The Lesson:

God is not distant nor unmoved when we hurt. God sees all who call upon His name. We can trust that our struggle is His classroom, and our pain His teacher, all being supervised under His watchful eye. "I will instruct you and teach you in the way which you should go; I will counsel you with My eye upon you" (Ps. 32:8).

Power Principle:

The Lord had graciously planned this camp meeting for me at one of the most desperate times of my life. The message for the depleted Christian was perfectly timed. I could not have gone on imitating the Christian life any more than a car could run on an empty tank. I needed Jesus to take up His life in mine. Life had beaten me, and I had no more strength left to fight—exactly where I needed to be to receive the good news of Jesus Christ in a totally different form. Not only was Jesus sent to earth to save me from my sins and give me eternal life, but at the moment, He offered His own mind, personality, and strength for me to live my life.

> I could not have gone on imitating the Christian life any more than a car could run on an empty tank. I needed Jesus to take up His life in mine.

Now I had an alternative way of thinking and living. Jesus could live the Christian life through me, like a hand in a glove, like gas in a car, like electricity in a lamp. Little by little I learned how to take a moment and breathe a prayer of "thank you" to God before every challenging situation and let Jesus live through me.

I also gained a new response system when I encountered harsh or disrespectful remarks from my husband. He gave me permission to ask him, "Is that Jesus speaking to me?" bringing immediate conviction. You can imagine the changes that come from living life with the awareness of Jesus in your midst. I began to listen to myself as well, knowing full well when it was my response or His. Knowing that I had God to rely on lifted the burden from my soul. I could now relax and let Jesus live an authentic Christian life through me, rather than rely on my cheap imitation. Together we could go back home and face whatever needed to be faced. This I believed with all my heart, and peace came flooding in.

Learning to trust in the Lord with all my heart stabilized my emotions and freed my mind to receive the powerful principles of prayer. Great lessons were wrapped in the mundane circumstances of life. I wouldn't realize until much later that I was in the process of learning about the revolutionary power of prayer.

ABCs of WordSpeak
A—Asking for God's Help

Truly, truly, I say to you, if you ask the Father for anything, He will give it to you in my name. Until now, you have asked for nothing in My name; ask, and you will receive.

—John 16:23–24

Chapter 4

Asking for Help

*If you abide in Me, and My words abide in you, ask whatever you
wish, and it shall be done for you.*

—John 15:7

Within the first year of our marriage, we got pregnant, bought and
sold a home, quit our jobs, started a business, and had a baby. Not
a business plan I would recommend. And yet, I remember telling God that if
He would work out all these impossible circumstances, I would gladly give my
testimony. I was forever saying things like that to manipulate God into doing
what I wanted. The Lord, with His inimitable sense of humor, usually kept me
to my end of the bargain, and there I'd be, shaking from my very core in front
of our Sunday school class, testifying to the amazing goodness of God.

Like the good Father He was, God was ever so patient with me during my
early sanctimonious days. Being raised in a preacher's home, I thought I knew
everything there was to know about
God and His ways. But God had to
draw me away from the protected walls
of the church to reveal Himself in my
everyday world. You can imagine my
surprise when none of the Sunday
school lessons seemed to work out in
my everyday world. God had a different
course for me than I had planned, one
that would give me a future and a hope

I learned to have conversations
with Him, and the most
astounding thing of all is
this—He listens to me.

that would stand up under the pressure of every day challenges. I didn't realize it then, but God was inviting me into His chambers, offering me a special relationship, one He offers to all of us. I learned to have conversations with Him, and the most astounding thing of all is this—He listens to me. "Then you will call upon Me and come and pray to Me, and I will listen to you" (Jer. 29:12).

Though WordSpeak is not intended to be a memoir, I invite you into my world, as chaotic as it was at times, to reveal the process God used to remold me and make me into a vessel of prayer. I spent many hours alone with Him, sitting at His knee, so to speak, hammering out the truth or falseness of what I believed about Him.

As a "mature" Christian, I had somehow skipped over the phase of being a child with my heavenly Father. So He took me back to the beginning, to learn my ABCs. I began my prayer life as all children do, begging Him for this and that. For me, A was learning it was okay to Ask my Father for Anything. "If you abide in Me, and My words abide

> I began my prayer life as all children do, begging Him for this and that. For me, A was learning it was okay to Ask my Father for Anything.

in you, ask whatever you wish, and it shall be done for you" (John 15:7).

I will never forget the day I warned the Lord, "You shouldn't have said this. People might take You literally."

As a young mother sequestered in my home every day with an infant, I was unable to make it to the women's Bible study at church. So I passed the time by memorizing key passages in the Bible. On this particular day, I tried to tackle John 15:7 during my baby's nap time. Distracted by my son John's vehement cries for his lost pacifier, I had a hard time concentrating, so I repeated the words out loud, "If you abide in Me and . . ."

Surely, he will exhaust himself and fall asleep. Oh, uh . . . "and My words abide in . . ." *Hmmm, already looked in the car, the baby bag . . . did I check his walker?*

No, not there. Just stay calm. Be determined. He can go to sleep on his own, the baby book says so. Okay, one more time, "If you abide in Me and My words . . ."

Gee, will he never give up? I had been working with him for forty-five minutes.

The last thing I saw before I gave up and went in again to calm him down were the words, "Ask whatever you wish, and it shall be done for you." No amount of rocking or singing or patting would do the trick. This kid wanted his pacifier and he was mad. Not about to be appeased, he arched his back frantically and almost threw himself out of my arms.

Placing him carefully back in his crib, I left the house one more time to search for the pacifier in the car. Perhaps he had dropped it on the sidewalk without my knowing. While I searched, these words began to crystallize in my mind, "Ask whatever you wish, and it shall be done for you."

"Okay, Lord," I whispered in faith, "you said I could ask for anything, so please show me where the pacifier is." Honestly, in that moment it felt more like a dare than a prayer. My nerves were on edge, and I decided I would give in, pick him up, and drive to the store to purchase another pacifier. To heck with the baby books!

I walked the sidewalk and perused the yard one more time, more to calm myself and get away from the poor baby's screams. Returning to the house, I heard these words as clear as a bell in my head, "Look in the mailbox." My heart took a little leap as I walked up to the house and opened the lid of my black mailbox beside the front door. I was almost too afraid to look, not wanting to be disappointed in God.

But there it was, plain as day. *How did it end up there? Who could have put it in there?* I wondered. I didn't stop to analyze but dashed off to put it in my baby's mouth. You can imagine the time of celebration the Lord and I had that afternoon as my son drifted off to a long nap. I was beside myself with joy. I believe God and I both got a good laugh from my first practical lesson in the power of prayer. "Truly, truly, I say to you, if you shall ask the Father for anything, He will give it to you in My name. Ask, and you will receive, that your joy may be made full" (John 16:23b, 24b).

I feel giddy when I think of someone daring to ask God for anything in Jesus' name.

It is time to let you in on a secret that is as audacious as it is wonderful. The words "truly, truly," mean that what Jesus was about to say is really important and we should take notice. I almost hold my breath each time I hear this verse read aloud, as if someone might misunderstand His promise "He will give it to you in My name." I feel giddy when I think of someone daring to ask God for anything in Jesus' name.

I can hear your arguments now. And yes, there are conditions and barriers. But before we get to that, let's enjoy the lavishness of this offer. Seeing the same promise repeated numerous times in the New Testament, I marvel at the great lengths God has gone to in order to invite us to ask Him for help in living.

The Lesson:

Jesus gave us permission to ask the Father about anything we need here on earth. The words *whatever*, *may*, and *anything* leave no room for doubt. "And I will do whatever you ask in my name, so that the Son may bring glory to the Father. You may ask me for anything in my name, and I will do it" (John 14:13–14 NIV).

Power Principle:

One of the conditions of answered prayer, "If you abide in Me, and my words abide in you," begs the question, just how are we to abide in Him? I knew all about Jesus, but I had not learned to abide in Him. Early on, I realized that though I knew a lot of stories about Jesus, I didn't know Him. So I decided to read through the New Testament to find out what He was like. There Jesus came alive to me, and I began to become aware of His presence. His words came to life and I took them personally, including Him in my life. I learned to abide in Him like a little child abides with a loving father, staying tucked under His strong arm in times of trouble or celebration, sharing with Him all the moments of my life.

> I learned to abide in Him like a little child abides with a loving father, staying tucked under His strong arm in times of trouble or celebration, sharing with Him all the moments of my life.

My advice for fulfilling the condition is this: Get to know Him by reading through the Gospels with an open heart. Don't simply rely on the lessons you've heard in church. Come to Him personally and privately. Sure, you can worship Him in public, but you get to be His friend in private. When you find yourself enjoying a pleasure in this world, enjoy it with Him. When you are disappointed, share it with Him. When you are afraid, turn to Him.

Most importantly, be yourself before God. Jesus said, "I and the Father are one" (John 10:30). Present your problems and your victories to Him without the pretense of religious-sounding words. God really does not speak the Elizabethan English of the King James Bible and it does not impress Him when we do. He probably wonders who He is talking to when we speak to him in a language not our own.

Simply memorizing a Bible verse ("and My words abide in you") is only a beginning. You must think about it and talk about it with God and others, asking this question, "How does this work in my life?" In time you will experience the assurance that a transformed mind brings as you test and prove the good, acceptable, and perfect will of God (Rom. 12:2). As you stay close to Him, pray with Him, read the Word with Him, and have His words implanted deep within, you will be able to ask Him for anything you wish and it shall be done for you because your desires will be shaped by His Word and His Spirit.

The first steps toward effective praying are to ask, acknowledge, and abide. By acknowledging God in all you do, asking Him for favors, and abiding in His Word, you will be amazed how quickly you understand His will.

Chapter 5

Asking for Healing

*If . . . my people who are called by my name humble themselves and
pray, and seek My face and turn from their wicked ways, then I will
hear from heaven, will forgive their sin, and heal their land.*

—2 Chronicles 7:14

Stan and I forged ahead as young couples do, fiercely fighting to earn a living. As the sole owner, my husband worked long hours to raise his infant business while I did the same with my infant son. Unfortunately, we also fell into the habit of fighting against each other as we wrestled with the aloneness of our endeavors. Because of our independent natures he did his thing and I did mine, not learning to become a team, instead allowing the demands of life to form a wedge between us.

On the good side, Stan had the financial backing of respected Christian businessmen in our prosperous and dynamic church. These successful men faithfully mentored Stan in the ways and means of a bull economy. Other than the estrangement of living life separately, we were moving into a bright future. Stan was also very active in our church, working tirelessly in various capacities. He was the golden boy, full of promise and energy. Living large in his alligator boots and cowboy hat, Stan took on the challenge of setting up a twenty-four hour prayer room at our large Baptist church.

Much to our amazement, business boomed and Stan was able to open his own offices. He bought the furniture and equipment and hired a secretary, all within the first three years of our marriage. Always a man of faith, he brought in a buddy of his, got on his knees in his new space, and dedicated the business to the Lord. Our ship sailed into the prosperous seas of Houston, Texas and the oil boom.

Then one day, oil prices crashed and the "black gold" lost much of its value. A deep recession whipped through our city like a Texas twister, and in its wake the drought of the eighties took hold. Of course, at the time, we didn't know what hit us and forged ahead, living on borrowed money and waiting for the next "big deal." All those tied to the oil-based economy faltered, and over the next eighteen months my husband's business brought in less than $17,000—it was a short life for a big venture. He would have to close his doors, leaving us holding a large bag of capital indebtedness.

During this turbulent time, our second son, Mark, was born and on the third day of his life he also crashed. His heart and respiration spun out of control. Delivering the news late that night, the doctor told me that Mark's heart was failing, his liver and spleen enlarged, and his lungs filling with fluid. He was in fact, in stage four of congestive heart failure, a critical condition. I understood completely, for the day before I sat beside the bed of my sweet grandmother, in the same hospital, down the hall, struggling to breathe due to congestive heart failure. Both were clinging to life.

When the doctor left me alone it was close to midnight. Stunned, I didn't know whom to call for at this point my husband and I were barely on speaking terms. He was at home alone, sleeping peacefully with my toddler. I lay back on the pillow of my hospital bed, recuperating from a caesarian birth, and planned the funeral of my infant son. The only question was, which funeral would I attend first.

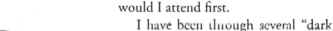

> Somehow I felt Stan and I were being punished for being the way we were, and what was happening to our son was our fault.

I have been through several "dark nights of the soul," but that night proved to be one of the darkest. Somehow I felt Stan and I were being punished for being the way we were, and what was happening to our son was our fault. I didn't even know how to pray so I lay there powerless and prayer-less. Finally, in the middle of the night, I picked up the phone and called my father.

As my father, my husband, and I looked at the fragile figure of my son in the incubator, I heard my father praying. My baby lay in an unnatural position, strapped down with needles and tubes inserted in each of his tiny limbs. A syringe was even inserted in the top of his head filling him with fluids giving his head a pointed, alien-like shape. Instead of a heartbeat, there was only a quiver in his chest. Instead of a cry, there was only a squeak coming from his mouth. Stan and I just sobbed at the frightful sight of him.

Back in my room, we began to wait out the night. All I remember was the heavy atmosphere of fear and the painful silence between us, and Stan lying there in the dark on the cot beside me with his boots still on.

There he lay tied up in an ICU incubator, awaiting his sentence—life or death.

The next few days were intense as Mark was transferred to the Texas Children's Heart Hospital. There he lay tied up in an ICU incubator, awaiting his sentence—life or death. The final prognosis was coarctation of

the aorta with a sizable hole in his left ventricle. We left him, stabilized and galvanized by heart medicines and went home to wait it out. We made many trips to and from the hospital to touch our delicate child.

Finally, after many days in ICU, we were told he could go home to await open-heart surgery. He was much too fragile for such a procedure, but at least he was stabilized. To make matters worse, further surgeries would be needed as he grew.

"Medicine has come a long way," my cousin, a resident in cardiology, said as he tried to comfort me. "Babies now have a fifty-fifty chance of surviving heart surgery." Seeing my eyes fill up with tears, he hurriedly added, "Ten years ago only ten percent survived."

While it didn't sound like good news to me, I simply held my breath and waited out the next few weeks as a remarkable story unfolded. Leaving our baby to the care of Texas Children's Hospital, I went home to recuperate and care for my young son, John.

Meanwhile, a large army of prayer warriors mobilized as the prayer room of my father's church, Tallowood Baptist, and its fledgling offspring, the prayer room of Second Baptist, went to work. Both prayer rooms had twenty-four hour staffs of seasoned pray-ers. Prayers for our son, Mark, went up around the clock. There can be no other explanation for the astounding news we received many days after our ordeal began.

One evening at dinnertime, the cardiologist called to explain that they noticed a change in the newest battery of tests on Mark. Perhaps they had made a mistake, he told us, but the coarctation of the artery could no longer be seen. He assured us he had ordered another scan to be sure. His condition was upgraded, and we could make plans to take him home. We could hardly take it in. Later I was admitted to the hospital to learn how to care for a "heart" baby before he was discharged, and the doctors came in to deliver conflicting reports.

The teaching doctor with his residents in tow gave a remarkable admission. "There must have been a mistake in the initial three rounds of echocardiograms because this type of congenital defect doesn't automatically resolve without surgery. It doesn't just go away on its own."

"So what about his blue arms and legs and face?" I asked nervously.

"Mark still has a ventricle septum defect and will have to stay on heart medicines," the doctor explained.

"Will the hole in his heart close on its own?" I asked.

"Not usually. Most holes this size require surgery." But then with a wink, he said to me, "But I doubt this kid will have any trouble with such a little thing as a hole in his heart."

And then he sent us home with prescriptions for everything except our own anxious hearts. Though we had some rough years, our baby made sure and steady progress and was released from cardiology care by the age of two. It wasn't until four years later during a hospital stay for a totally different illness that I became convinced of the miraculous healing of Mark's heart. A new cardiologist was brought in, putting Mark through another battery of tests, only to conclude his heart was perfectly normal.

"Then why all the tests?" I asked.

"Well, his history is so strange, we had to be sure we hadn't overlooked something. A baby doesn't stay in heart failure for two months without a good reason. But now we know he is okay, and that's what matters." "Moreover, I will give you a new heart and put a new spirit within you; and I will remove the heart of stone from your flesh and give you a heart of flesh" (Ezek. 36:26).

> God is still in the business of miracles. We cannot deny it, nor can we be afraid to pray for miracles.

Our story has a wonderful ending, and I almost hesitate to tell it, knowing the pain of many others whose stories have not ended so well. I feel a bit sheepish as I tell the wonderful events of Mark's life, but there is a lesson for all of us here. God is still in the business of miracles. We cannot deny it, nor can we be afraid to pray for miracles. I was the recipient of this miracle even though I was too entrenched in the battle for my son's life to pray. I felt too unworthy to ask for his life and healing. I was wrong. Thankfully, my ignorance did not stand in the way of God moving on Mark's behalf. I believe the outcry of His people was so great that He moved in answer to their cries. "Because their outcry has become so great before the Lord" (Gen. 19:13).

The Lesson:

When God's people cry out in unison and humility, God promises to hear from heaven and heal their land. In unison, the church forms a mighty army that marches against the enemy's schemes. "Upon this rock I will build My church; and the gates of hell will not prevail against it" (Matt. 16:18b KJV).

Power Principle:

You may be a parent whose heart breaks as you read my story because your child is crippled or handicapped in some way. This is a great mystery. I do not believe that God is the cause of this misery for you and your child. In fact, the gospel tells a completely different story of the compassion of Jesus. As God's heart toward kids was then, I believe His heart is now. He is the same today as He was yesterday when He walked on the earth. "And all the people were trying to touch Him, for power was coming from Him and healing them all" (Luke 6:19). Why would His heart change in this matter?

I also know God works out His great purposes within suffering. I would not add to your difficulties by suggesting that this is your fault. This subtle lie from the enemy places the responsibility for healing on us and is simply not true.

What is true is that the ASK process is available to all of us, no matter how impossible our circumstances. As you move through the process of asking, seeking, and knocking, God will reveal how you are to pray as you draw closer to Him. He will also give you the measure of faith needed as you pray through your problem. Our responsibility is to first acknowledge God in all our circumstances, and

As you pray according to the principles set out in His Word, you will experience all types of victories. Some victories come when difficult circumstances do not change, but attitudes do.

then ask to know His will. When you take God's Word and pray it over your cares, you are leaning on Him. As you pray according to the principles set out in His Word, you will experience all types of victories. Some victories come when difficult circumstances do not change, but attitudes do.

As believers, we are an army. It is our duty to come together to intercede on behalf of one another. That is how we go to war. I believe God honored the many hours of labor my husband spent organizing and inaugurating the Second Baptist prayer room. Ironically, it was newly inaugurated when my son was born. Perhaps the battle was won because the warriors were in place and prepared for such a crisis. The first move we made when confronted with this crisis was to call the prayer rooms, and they went to work on our behalf, acknowledging God as our hope for healing.

God instituted the church to be a powerful agent of change in this crippled, lightless world. Our testimony that Jesus is the Savior and all-powerful King, the Holy Spirit is the change agent, and God Almighty is our Father is the foundation upon which the church stands as we storm the gates of hell. We did, and in this instance, the body of Christ won.

Chapter 6

Asking for Provision

*Be anxious for nothing, but in everything by prayer and supplication,
with thanksgiving let your requests be made known to God. And the
peace of God, which surpasses all comprehension, will guard your hearts
and your minds in Christ Jesus.*

—Philippians 4:6–7

The years after the miracle of our son's healing were up and down. Though we were changed by the experience, it is amazing how the incessant stresses of life can cause God's power and availability to grow dim. Our miracle with Mark had to be walked out every day. It took years for us to relax concerning his health. We struggled to stay afloat under the mounting medical costs and the debts due to the financial collapse of Stan's business. Anxiety always lurked in the background, ready to ambush at any moment.

Another month had come and gone and there was not enough money to pay all the bills and feed my two little boys. God surprised us with another pregnancy. In my mind I would never have chosen to bring another baby into our chaotic world. I struggled to stay emotionally stable, and each morning I awoke with a knot in my stomach. I knew God's opinion on anxiety

No amount of telling myself not to worry got the job done. The message was not getting through to my central nervous system.

and conscientiously tried to keep it at bay by quoting the above passage in Philippians.

Quoting it aloud while I was at the sink preparing dinner, I stopped in exasperation and prayed, "Lord, I know this verse, but still I have no peace. I've got the words in my mind, but could You get the message to my stomach?" No amount of telling myself not to worry got the job done. The message was not getting through to my central nervous system. Once again I talked through the verse, carefully saying each word, when I was arrested by the phrase "let your requests be made known to God." Suddenly I realized I had never really heard the word "request" before.

"Request?!" I said with an emerging thought. When I was a secretary and needed new supplies, I submitted my requisition list to get the supplies needed to do my job. I was not embarrassed or hesitant in the least to ask for such needs. It would have been stupid not to ask. So God was telling me it was okay to submit my requisition list to Him just like I had done as a secretary.

> I was arrested by the phrase "let your requests be made known to God." Suddenly I realized I had never really heard the word "request" before.

"Okay, then," I said with assurance, "here is my requisition list. I need money to pay the light bill, and the water bill, and in case You didn't notice, we are having scrambled eggs for dinner." Oddly enough, a certain peace accompanied my prayer as if my helplessness had been obliterated by acting on my newfound discovery of God's truth. I was combining spiritual thoughts with spiritual words.

Not long after dinner I heard a knock at my front door. A friend of ours came in looking for my husband (who was gone to his second job). I was so sure he had fallen on hard times like so many of our friends that I took it on myself to "minister" to this man in my husband's stead. After the initial pleasantries, he asked me how we were doing.

"Well, we're all living hand to mouth, aren't we?" I answered.

"I know times have been tough for you guys. We've had some tough times ourselves, but you and Stan will come out of this a better man and woman," Gary said. He continued to speak knowingly of how difficulties build character.

"Yes, well, my husband says that, too, but," I told him, "I don't want any more character, I just want some cold cash in my hot little hand," I said, holding out my hand as a way of illustration. In one fluid motion he reached out and put something in my open hand and said that was the purpose of his visit. Completely taken by surprise, I didn't at first understand that he had given me a check. Horrified at my beggarly attempt at humor, I tried to give the check back to him. "No, no, really," I stammered, "I wasn't asking for money; I was just trying to make you feel better."

"What?" he asked, stumped.

"Aren't you out of a job?" I feebly tried to explain.

"No, I am doing well. But there was a time that I was in great need and someone gave this money to me with the stipulation that I pass it along to someone else in need. So you and Stan can do the same one day."

I was dumbfounded. When he left, I cried, embarrassed, relieved, humiliated, grateful, and amazed at the swiftness of God's answer to my prayer at the sink. This lesson, as much a lesson in humility as in anything else, was dramatic in its timing. Oh, and by the way, the amount of the check covered just enough for the light bill and the water bill with some left over for food. "And if we know He hears us in whatever we ask, we know that we have the requests which we have asked from Him" (1 John 5:14b–15).

Who knew we could make our requests known to the Lord? The Bible tells me so. Here it says that we will have the requests we ask from Him if we ask according to His will. Asking anything according to His will gets easier when we hang our prayers on the promises found in the Scriptures. By taking my problems to the Bible, I became acquainted with God's promises in practical matters. With each trial that presented itself to us, God challenged me to take it to heart or take it to Him.

> Asking anything according to His will gets easier when we hang our prayers on the promises found in the Scriptures.

The Lesson:

God is responsible for causing His Word to become reality in the ways and means He wishes. I certainly can give God my requests, but He is the provider. "My God shall supply all your needs according to His riches in glory in Christ Jesus" (Phil. 4:19).

Power Principle:

In our WordSpeak Way Prayer Square (a prayer group limited to four people), we have an interesting approach to presenting our requests to God.

We come up with the most pressing desire or need of the person we are praying for. Someone else brings the requests to God by lifting up their hands as if serving the requests on a platter. We jokingly say, "It's your turn to get on the platter." We do this to visualize our requests as something tangible and doable.

This exercise is not as easy as it sounds. Each of us is forced to think deeply about what is truly bothering us and present our requests in their most relevant and reduced form. Many times we have to help one another get more specific. Furthermore, most everyone feels dubious about the right to ask for specifics at first.

But just think of how frustrated the waiter would feel if you were to respond to his question, "What would you like to eat?" with this:

"I'm feeling hungry, so I want something that is satisfying."

Surely he would respond, "Could you be more specific?"

Because I relied on God to know what was best for me, I had lost touch with the desires of my heart. I have a hard time letting my requests be made known to anyone, much less to God. Living under the assumption that I would receive the desires of my heart without so much as a peep from me seemed normal and reasonable. My desires were a happy, peaceful home with people who could pay their bills and were nice to one another. I also expected life to be fun, which it decidedly had not been. It never occurred to me to voice my desires in specific terms. That went against everything in me.

But clearly the verse on anxiety says to make your requests known to God. My wise counselor has often said to relieve yourself of anxiety you must give it words. By giving words to what is bothering you, you lessen the effects of anxiety.

In our prayer square it was difficult to do this at first, because we were so out of touch with our emotions. But once we stopped and thought about it, we could verbalize our discomfort. Sometimes the thought processes behind the anxiety were laughable, but once we expressed ourselves to the group, what was at the bottom of the trouble became clear. Once we cleaned away the debris and rested on the one thing that might be causing our anxiety, we discovered our request. Most often the challenge was to believe God or the lies we held so closely.

God has given us the right and responsibility to make our requests known to Him. Not only is it an excellent exercise in self-discovery, it enables us to partner with God. He then trades our worries for the peace of God that guards our hearts and minds. Now that is a good trade.

Chapter 7

Asking for Blessing

The Lord bless you, and keep you; the Lord make His face shine on you, and be gracious to you.

—Numbers 6:24–25

For years, I lived a voiceless life, not knowing how to ask anything for myself. I equated being nice with not asking. Being nice had its benefits, but for me it became a deadly performance that demoralized my being and allowed bad conditions to stay in my life. God gives each of us a voice for a reason. Having been trained to go along with the flow, I did not realize that my purpose and future were tied to my ability to speak up. I had a sweet mother who rarely criticized or voiced her opinion, and I felt it was my job to do the same.

As a matter of necessity, a tough covering encased my heart in the face of the distresses of my troubled life. I remember sitting in front of my bedroom window so depressed I had not dressed for the day. We had just returned from a weekend with my husband's family where I had witnessed the stark reality of kids who were treated with the harshness of unkind dog owners.

Anger and bitterness broke through to my conscious self and I experienced the icy fingers of hatred choking my throat.

Anger and bitterness broke through to my conscious self and I experienced the icy fingers of hatred choking my throat. Nothing could have felt more wrong to me, but neither could I keep these feelings suppressed any longer. As I stared out the window I said aloud, "God, I know it's wrong to be filled with so much hate, but I don't even care. I need You to work in me to 'will and do Your good pleasure' because I don't even have the will to want to." Then out of sadness for my little family, a curious prayer rushed from my heart.

"God, bless this family with happiness! There has been too much sadness. I wrestle with You like Jacob did the angel, and I won't let go until You bless us." And then I heard my voice speak in an unfamiliar way, "And I don't want to have to accept by faith that You've heard me. I need a real flesh and blood answer." I had never felt so determined. This was the cry of a wounded heart, not the nice behavior of the good little Christian girl who would never ask for anything selfish. The intensity of my pain overrode my restrained manners with God. I was a desperado.

This was the cry of a wounded heart, not the
nice behavior of the good little Christian girl who would never ask for anything selfish.

I don't know how long I sat there staring out the window, but when I was finally able to dislodge myself, I turned around, startled to see my husband leaning on the doorframe of our bedroom door. Embarrassed to be in such a state, I brusquely asked him what he was doing home in the middle of the morning.

"I don't know," he answered, "basically obeying the nudging of the Holy Spirit. He told me to come home. There's something I need to say to you and the boys."

Yeah, I bet, I said to myself. But he did have something to say, and no amount of cynicism could deny that what happened was nothing short of a miracle.

In his quiet time, the Lord had shown my husband a picture of what his angry upbringing was doing to our family and godly sorrow had broken his heart. He simply wanted to say he was sorry and ask us to forgive him. He gathered us around the kitchen table and told the boys how his anger had hurt Mommy and them.

First he asked our little boys, ages four and two-and-a-half, to forgive him, and then he asked me. "It's okay, Daddy," I heard them say sweetly, but I was too stunned to answer. I had become hardened to his apologies, but this was different.

He was eager to read to us the verses that had convicted him that morning, but I stopped him with the excuse that the boys were too young. In reality, I was not ready to listen to him "preach" one thing and behave another. *If you must*, I thought hardheartedly, and I handed him a children's devotional book. He turned to the devotion for that day, and guess what? There on the page, written in a the living language a child could understand, were the very verses on anger that had brought conviction to his heart. We were both shocked by the precision and presence of the Lord.

I will always remember that day as a morning of many miracles, but the most precious was when my husband bowed his head and prayed, "Lord, forgive me for the anger that has done so much harm to Mommy and John and Mark. Change me. Help me break this cycle of anger in my life. Let it stop with me." And then with intensity, voice quivering, I heard him pray a determined prayer, "And Lord, bless this family with happiness! I'm wrestling with you, God, like Jacob did. I won't let go till you bless us!"

At a time when I couldn't speak for myself, the Word of God spoke for me.

There it was. My flesh and blood answer. God had heard the cry of my wounded heart and confirmed it through the mouth of my husband. My heart began to thaw, and though repair would take some time, I had no trouble forgiving that day. My husband began a lifelong battle to win against the anger and hurt within himself and has remained steadfastly faithful to pray for our family throughout it all. I have no doubt that because of his continued prayers we have experienced so much blessing.

God helped me by putting His words in my mouth, "Behold, I have put My words in your mouth" (Jer. 1:12). At a time when I couldn't speak for myself, the Word of God spoke for me. I believe the prayers God generated that day became the words of our mouths when we both prayed, "Bless this family with happiness."

Though I didn't understand it fully, I knew the story of Jacob wrestling with the angel. My husband and I came into agreement through our prayers without even knowing it, and God has continued to bless this family with happiness.

The Lesson:

If you hide God's Word in your heart, He will put His words in your mouth when you most need them. "The Spirit of the Lord spoke by me, and His word was on my tongue" (2 Sam. 23:2).

Power Principle:

One of the most powerful prayers we can pray is the prayer for God's blessing. Not only is it proper to pray for a blessing on your own life, but it is modeled over and over in Scripture. Once your eyes are opened to the concept of praying good things into your life and those of others, you will begin to see many prayers of blessings in the Bible. The WordSpeak Prayer Cards called "Blessings" will get you started on a life of blessing others.

By praying a blessing or speaking a blessing, you are co-laboring with God to bring His goodness into this world.

You may be unaware of the power of blessing, but every one of us carries out this transference of God's goodness to one another when we offer a simple, "Good morning" to those we pass. A blessing is simply the utterance of a wish or request that good will come into someone's life. Once you connect to God, you connect to the divine source of blessing. By praying a blessing or speaking a blessing, you are co-laboring with God to bring His goodness into this world.

"Bless those who persecute you; bless and curse not" (Rom. 12:14). Blessing those who persecute us brings peace into our lives, because when our enemies are blessed, they are more likely to live at peace with us. By praying for God's blessings to be poured out on earth, we help to bring His order to this world. Therefore, we need to become more intentional in praying for and giving blessings to those around us, especially our children.

Whenever I part with my loved ones, I most often speak this blessing over them, "May God bless your comings and your goings," a prayer based on Psalm 121. The first step in living a life of blessing is to accept the reality of God's wish that we ask Him for favors. His goodness will flow into our the world through our prayers and our words of blessings. What a simple yet awesome responsibility.

Chapter 8

Asking for Wisdom

But if any of you lacks wisdom, let him ask of God, who gives to all
men generously and without reproach, and it will be given to him.

—James 1:5

One of my first lessons in applying what we had learned at CBMC family camp came in the trenches of parenting a preschooler just days after returning. I had dealt with the same problem over and over again. Each time I was left feeling frustrated with myself and furious with my little daughter. She was too young to have such strong opinions about what she wore. Her definite opinions began at a very early age and I was tired of buying clothes for her that she later refused to wear.

I read the psychology books and laid out choices for her on the bed. I took her with me when she was four years old, as absurd as that sounds, to make sure the clothes we bought didn't offend her sensibilities. Sunday mornings were particularly treacherous. I was ready to pull my hair out as well as a strand or two from her head!

One day, I walked away from the skirmish to gain my composure, and simply prayed, "Thank You, Lord, that You have promised to act in me. Please give me wisdom. I need a boatload of heavenly advice about now!"

The answer came inside my head as I walked down the hall past her room. "Give the clothes to Angelina," was all I heard. Looking out of the large dining room window, I saw Angelina, a thin, poorly dressed little girl who had been abandoned by her mother, lying in the grass on the front lawn of my neighbor, a day-care provider. I was stunned at the immediacy of the answer, but slowly the brilliance of the wisdom hit me. Of course! I could teach my daughter a valuable lesson as well as feel good about offering the clothes to someone who would really appreciate them.

"That's brilliant!" I cried out to God, knowing that this would do the trick and cause my daughter to want the clothes after all. I proceeded to carry out the plan but stopped short at the door to her room with a very important follow-up question. "So, what if my daughter decides she wants them?" I asked the Lord.

"Give them to Angelina anyway," I heard in my mind as clear as a bell. Suddenly, I realized I didn't really want to give away the clothes I had bought on my very tight budget. I so wanted my daughter to look pretty like the other little girls at church with bows in their hair. But there was no equivocating now. I had asked for wisdom and my Father in heaven, the greatest parent of all, had given it.

I informed my daughter that we would give the clothes to Angelina, and you guessed it. She wanted them for sure. But I had no problem following through in spite of her tears because I knew this wisdom was from above. From that point, if she ever changed her mind and didn't want to wear her clothes, we always had the option of giving them to Angelina. "The wisdom from above is first pure, then peaceable, gentle, reasonable, full of mercy and good fruits, unwavering, without hypocrisy" (James 3:17).

Our responsibility is to ask God for wisdom when discerning direction for our lives. A true understanding of God's generosity toward us as His children removes any doubt that God hears us when we pray. I don't know whose lesson was more important that day—mine or my daughter's—but I learned a thing or two. When I call, He is ready to answer. I had better be ready to hear and obey.

The Lesson:

I can ask God for wisdom when I don't know what to do and He will gladly give it to me, as much as I need. "The LORD hears when I call to Him" (Ps. 4:3).

Power Principle:

If you say, "I don't know His will in this matter," you simply need to read His Last Will and Testament, the Bible. Confidence in prayer comes once you know His will. Your responsibility is to discover as best you can what He wants to do in your situation. In the WordSpeak prayer products we have compiled some key scriptures and placed them together in categories to get you started. You do not have to go through life like a blind man walking through an obstacle course. You can ask for wisdom from above, which the Bible says is first pure, then peaceable, gentle, reasonable, full of mercy and good fruits, unwavering, without hypocrisy that will reap peace. This is a tall order. You will know you have His answer when your heart settles down and feels peaceful.

Wisdom from above is truly a gift from God and we have been given an open invitation to ask for it. It is one of the rights and privileges of being a child of God. We must let go of the lie that God is hiding something from us. When you do not know what to pray, or how to proceed, simply ask for His wisdom. Declare aloud, "I can ask God for wisdom when I don't know what to do and He will gladly give it to me, as much as I need." Repeat it as many times as you need to begin to believe it. Then watch expectantly for God to deliver, and don't worry, you won't miss it.

You will know you have His answer when your heart settles down and feels peaceful.

We must let go of the lie that God is hiding something from us.

ABCs of WordSpeak
B—Belief That Behaves

And all things you ask in prayer, believing, you shall receive.

—Matthew 21:22

Chapter 9

Believing God's Word

*For I know whom I have believed and I am convinced that He is able
to guard what I have entrusted to Him until that day.*

—2 Timothy 1:12

The next stage of my growth came as God began to challenge me to take Him at His Word. Was I going to remain a child or was I going to learn to believe by faith the promises of God? This lesson began my son's first day of school. As a young mother I was hopeful about all the possibilities available to him as he stepped out of our home and into the world. With high hopes and some trepidation, I took John to find his classroom and meet his teacher. You can imagine my dismay as I entered John's classroom to find it filled with children who could barely speak English. The school had been re-districted to include an apartment complex that was home for many immigrants.

My eyes quickly scanned the classroom to find a potential friend for John. Surely I could find someone who spoke English. After orientation, I followed the only other blonde boy to meet his parents. You can imagine my chagrin when he walked up to a young lady with bleach-blonde hair wearing black fishnet stockings and a short leather skirt to kindergarten orientation!

> *Great. The only other English-speaking boy in his class and his mother is a hooker!* I thought darkly.

Great. The only other English-speaking boy in his class and his mother is a hooker! I thought darkly. The next morning after dropping him off, I became so disturbed I decided to march back to school, withdraw my son, and enroll him in a private school. Before I left, I went through the motions of asking for God's will in this matter. Honestly, I was doing more of "pitching a fit" before the throne than asking for God's help with the decision.

"All my friends have their kids in private Christian schools," I "prayed." As I picked up my purse and started to walk out the door, the thought hit me, *I suppose I ought to give God a little time to answer.* So I sat back down on my bed and picked up my *Daily Light,* a devotional book of scriptures compiled for each day. But my mind was already made up. Setting my car keys aside in order to turn the pages, I found the reading for September 4. Immediately, the words hit me squarely in the face:

> Sit still, my daughter.
> Be careful, keep calm and don't be afraid.
> Do not lose heart. Be still and know that I am God.
> Did I not tell you that if you believed,
> you would see the glory of God?
> Commune on your bed, search your heart and be silent.
> Be still before the Lord and wait patiently for him;
> The one who trusts will never be dismayed.

Loosely translated, the Lord was saying to me, "Hold your horses there, sister! I have a few things to say."

My bravado melting, I began to speak honestly to God. "But how will I face my (more prosperous) friends who think I am a terrible mother for sending my child to public school?" His answer came quickly as I continued to read:

> The arrogance of man will be brought low and the
> pride of men humbled; the Lord alone will be exalted in
> that day.
> Mary . . . sat at Jesus' feet, and heard his word.
> In returning and rest shall you be saved;
> in quietness and in confidence shall be your strength.
> He that believes shall not make haste.

It dawned on me that I was having an intimate conversation with the Lord of the universe. His Word spoke to me as clearly as if He were sitting in the room. Crumpling into a position of submission, I cried, knowing an answer

I did not want to hear had come. Once the emotions emptied, a peace swept over my soul. My son would be okay. I had His Word on it. And that would make all the difference.

Those words from the Lord became an anchor for me in the next few years of John's elementary education. I did not remove him from the public school system, and through the years I saw in many ways God moved on his behalf. His kindergarten teacher earned "Teacher of the Year" because of her loving, nurturing, creative approach. The next three years his teachers were Christians whom we knew in our church. He was pulled out of the mainstream classroom on many occasions and given special attention, eventually being placed in the gifted program. Best of all, he met a beautiful immigrant boy in the fifth grade and they became friends in spite of the language barrier. That young boy, through John's influence, has grown to be a dedicated Christian, serving the Lord with his beautiful wife in a bilingual ministry. They hope to take the good news back to their country one day.

> It dawned on me that I was having an intimate conversation with the Lord of the universe. His Word spoke to me as clearly as if He were sitting in the room.

The Word of God spoke clearly to me, and my attitude had to line up with God's will. Not without its challenges, John's education was much more than sufficient. This experience proved to me that I wasn't alone in the rearing of my child. Because I yielded to His words that day, and left John in that school, I believe God's purposes were carried out in his life. John has grown to have a passion for people of other nations, traveling to many countries carrying the good news of Jesus Christ. He and a group of dynamic young businessmen raised forty thousand dollars to join with Christian leaders in Haiti to pray for the transformation of their country. And by the way, he speaks fluently the language of those kids who outnumbered him that first day in kindergarten. "Your word is a lamp to my feet, and a light to my path" (Ps. 119:105).

During frustrating moments, I hear myself say, "Just give it to me straight, Lord." Rarely do we get immediate answers in critical decision-making moments. I believe God wants to grow us up into mature decision-makers, and simply telling us what to do at each step keeps us immature. But when we open our minds to His Word, we give Him the opportunity to speak to us, guide us, and train us in His timing, according to His purposes.

The Lesson:

Taking the time to hear God's voice not only brings us the assurance that He hears our cry, but also brings the direction for our lives. "The entrance of Your words gives light; it gives understanding to the simple" (Ps. 119:130).

Every prayer you pray initiates a conversation with God the Father. You should expect an answer.

Power Principle:

Every prayer you pray initiates a conversation with God the Father. You should expect an answer. You listen by opening your consciousness to God and reading His Word. You must not disrespect Him by failing to listen to Him in return or by demanding instant answers. Keep in mind that He is the boss. Most often we pray as if we do not expect to hear Him answer. After an impression comes it must be filtered through the Word of God.

Addressing Him as "Father" displays an attitude of submission and trust. It is bad manners to begin making conversation or requests before acknowledging someone's presence. Yet so often we treat God disrespectfully by uttering prayers that sound more like a child barging into a room, declaring his demands.

Yet so often we treat God disrespectfully by uttering prayers that sound more like a child barging into a room, declaring his demands.

You must enter prayer with an open heart to receive from God any communiqués He might want to give you. In order to hear, you must be willing to listen. Reading the Bible and a daily devotion book is the best way to hear God's answers. We often forget that prayer is a two-way conversation. Bring an attitude of humility and a willingness to be a learner. When you sincerely say, "Lord, teach me to hear You," you open the door to real communication with God.

The second step is much more difficult—choosing to believe after God speaks. Once you see an answer or a promise that seems to be applicable to your prayer concern you now have a choice—to believe or not to believe? That is the question. We want to hear God speak to us about our concern, but we are not sure what His voice sounds like. We are more likely to recognize God's voice when we have His words in our mind.

When you sincerely say, "Lord, teach me to hear You," you open the door to real communication with God.

When the answer comes and you feel doubtful, simply ask God if a particular verse or spiritual thought is true for you. He is not offended if you need Him to restate it. Occasionally I hear a statement on the radio, television, or in a movie and I feel as if God is speaking directly to my problem. Recently, during a time of scary decision-making, I saw a large billboard displaying two words, "BE BRAVE!" The experience so resonated with my emotions that I had no doubt believing it was a "sign" from the Lord.

Even so, I read the Bible expectantly, waiting to hear a word of confirmation. When the answer comes, and eventually it does, I stand on that word and begin to pray for it to come true in my life or in the life of the one I am praying for.

All those words given to me so long ago did come to pass in John's life. Was his time at that school all peaches and cream? Probably not, although I remember it as being a good time. God's promises take time to come to pass. We must believe Him in the beginning and align our attitudes with the fact that God is true to His Word. Then as the journey unfolds our hearts will have peace watching His purposes come to pass.

Chapter 10

A Belief That Behaves

Faith by itself, if it is not accompanied by action, is dead.

—James 2:17 (NIV)

Looking back over the early days of my experiences in the "school of prayer," I can pinpoint a very few times when I made a conscious choice to believe God and act on one of His promises. Most of the time, I was simply learning to lean on Him and hanging on for dear life. But the Holy Spirit was an active tutor, pulling me along, drawing me into the Scriptures, handing me challenges to choose to believe God or one of the threatening circumstances that constantly seemed to be breathing down our necks.

My learning experience was predictable. Circumstances came first, then a time of chaos, then a time of searching for God's will. But always it came down to this: what was I going to believe about God's faithfulness? At the time, I did not understand the importance of belief in the prayer process. I was growing in confidence in God's nearness and concern and in His inclination to work in my circumstances with each passing victory, but belief is a step beyond confidence. True belief demands an action.

I distinctly remember the first time I consciously acted in faith. It was a frightening time for us. Stan was self-employed, our life was held hostage to the commission-based pay system. We could never be sure where the next paycheck was coming from. That simply meant we had to wait until a deal closed, business payments were made, Uncle Sam was considered, and then we received whatever was left.

The process of his work was precarious. He could put in hours of labor, only to have a deal fall apart at the last minute. This time, after spending eighteen months on a solid transaction, we both became convinced that his commission would steady us for a while. Even I began to feel hopeful and make plans. Not having insurance, I had left my health issue unattended for a long time. But now Stan and I could see the light at the end of a long, dark tunnel, and so I mustered up the courage to make an appointment with a doctor who offered a hopeful regimen for the chronic illness I had been dealing with for several years. I finally took some steps to get the help I needed.

A year and a half of engineering, devising, organizing, planning, managing, orchestrating—all went down the drain in a matter of minutes.

However, during the final negotiations, it became obvious to all involved that the buyer, whom Stan represented, was not able to come up with the required amount of money. A year and a half of engineering, devising, organizing, planning, managing, orchestrating—all went down the drain in a matter of minutes. I was astonished that such a thing could happen. Why had the client let it go this far? How could my husband not have seen this coming?

But indignation and outrage wouldn't feed the kids or pay the medical expenses. It was too late to cancel my appointment but it took everything in me just to go. My propensity for not asking for help was deeply entrenched and merely going to the appointment was an act of faith. I listened to the doctor's extensive proposition to build up my immune system to help fight a disease that no one seemed to understand. A necessary change of diet, along with a combination of vitamins and medicines, would be involved.

Of course, more doctor visits, blood tests, and frequent shots were undertaken to try to make any headway with the disorder that had caused chronic aseptic hepatitis, along with a medley of accompanying symptoms—malaise, inability to eat, hives, swollen glands, disorientation, fevers, rashes, swelling, etc. I was a physical and psychological mess. I was living a half-life, unable to enjoy either life or family. More than once waves of quiet desperation made me feel my family would be better off with me dead.

Seeing the resignation and discouragement in my eyes and my slow movements, this Christian doctor gave me a pep talk about his unorthodox treatment that involved medicinal, spiritual, and nutritional aspects. I still remember this point in his lecture:

"So many Christians are walking around in such an unhealthy physical state that they don't have their brain energy they need to function in the gifts of the Spirit. By ignoring the principles of health we limit our brain's ability to exhibit the fruits of the Spirit, and thus we are a poor advertisement to the world."

How true, how true, I thought. I was so listless, I couldn't muster up a good dose of joy to save a mouse, much less a neighbor. So upon hearing the good doctor's approach, I felt a bit of hope. Perhaps God had after all led me in the right direction. My good spirits lasted all the way to the pharmacy where I was hit with a bill for $450! I walked out of the pharmacy without the medicine, feeling a deadening blow to my emotions. I sat for a while in my car, confused as to what to do.

By ignoring the principles of health we limit our brain's ability to exhibit the fruits of the Spirit, and thus we are a poor advertisement to the world.

Hadn't God led me in this direction? Didn't I feel a sense of hopefulness for the first time in years? Was this a cruel trick of God—dangling the carrot of hope only to dash it immediately? Feeling dazed, I simply drove home, not allowing myself the luxury of letting the tears flow. Besides, I was numb to disappointment, which seemed to be my closest companion.

My husband's response was, "Just get the medicine. We'll figure it out. Your health is more important." But I felt it was a choice between medicines or food for my kids. How could a mother make that choice? Living with an upper middle-class mentality, we didn't think to avail ourselves of governmental assistance. Once more, I felt trapped in a never-ending cycle of frustration.

However, a wonderful lesson was about to unfold. The promises I found in the Scriptures had been speaking loudly to me throughout these difficult years, and it was time for my so-called beliefs to take action.

The moment of decision is clear in my mind. I remember where I was when I gathered the courage to go back to the pharmacy and write the check to pay for the much needed medicines and nutritional aids. I sat in the parking lot for quite some time, gathering my nerve. This time I gave myself a pep talk, trying to convince myself that it would be okay to write this check.

"You said You would take care of me," I said aloud to God in the car. "You said You would provide. I know You want me to get well. By faith I'm going to write this check, and I just pray You'll take care of this."

I'm not sure if I was asking God to cover the check or what. I remember the struggle to make the choice to take action, based on my belief, as weak as it was, that God would provide. It was time for me to put my health in God's hands. There seemed to be no going back. I had to cross the line and walk through those doors because belief was calling for action.

A good ending to this story would be that the check did not bounce and we went on our normal way of living and paying. But bless the Lord, He wanted to make sure I remembered this moment. So to make a point, the Lord moved in someone's heart to write us a note of encouragement that said:

"Dear Stan and Laura, God put your name on my heart this morning. Seems like you might need this for something. God bless, Truitt Lively."

Included in the note was a check for five hundred dollars. It came in the mail three days after I wrote the check to the pharmacy.

The Lesson:

If evidence demands a verdict, then belief demands an action. Faith without works is not really faith. "Even so, faith, if it has no works, is dead, being by itself" (James 2:17).

Power Principle:

"Prove it!" The words of that childhood dare ring in my ear as I think about this verse. If you say God is good, then prove it by your actions. If you say you believe God is faithful, then stake your life—and your money—on it. Abraham staked the life of his only son on this belief that God was good, and if he were called to sacrifice his only son, there had to be a good reason. He probably believed that God would raise Isaac from the dead. As Abraham raised the knife to kill his son, an angel stopped him and told him that God had provided a substitute, a ram found in a nearby thicket.

Though our sacrifices tend not to be this extreme, each of us must back our beliefs with some form of action. I believe so strongly in the airplane's ability to take off and land safely that I actually buy a ticket and board the plane. We say we have faith, and yet many times our actions do not bear out our beliefs.

Human error can so easily be involved in this process of acting on faith that much prayer and counsel needs to be involved as well. I believe we can still take the medicine prescribed for an illness and stand in faith for healing. We must do our part to participate in the healing process, as well as obey scriptural protocol for prayers of healing. Waiting on the Lord and asking for His wisdom and guidance are vital prerequisites to taking steps of faith.

The question that stares each of us in the face is this: What actions have I taken recently that back up my belief in God's Word?

The process of believing the Scriptures and acting on them not only pleases God, it also keeps us from sinning. When I choose to believe in God's rule for sexual purity, my

actions will line up. When I choose to believe that God will protect and care for me, I lie down in peace. Small action steps begin very close to home as we learn to act on what the Bible says. The question that stares each of us in the face is this: What actions have I taken recently that back up my belief in God's Word?

Chapter 11

Believing That God Is Faithful

And Jesus said to the centurion, "Go; it shall be done for you as you have believed."

—Matthew 8:13

Along with many others in the oil and real estate businesses, my husband had to close down his office, leaving us with bills and leases we could not pay. Scrambling to put food on the table, my husband worked part-time for a Christian businessman who helped him negotiate his losses. The bank holding our commercial line of credit had been bought out and the new bank called for the full balance of $13,000 that we owed. Because we could not come up with the money, the bank was suing us. Having legally separated from his cosigner, Stan had to face the charges alone.

"Well, Mr. Bower, who is representing you?" the judge asked my husband, who stood that day without the benefit of counsel.

"No one, Sir, I am representing myself," he replied much to the judge's chagrin.

In the end, the gavel came down pronouncing a judgment against him and a lien on our house. In former times, my husband would have been carted off to debtor's prison. He walked out of the courtroom feeling the full weight of his responsibilities, with a wife and three small children to feed, the IRS breathing down his neck, and hospital bills to pay.

Stan and I went to all the resources we could find to ask for a loan, each one replying that with all our debts, it was too much to ask. He went to his financial institutions, and I went to mine. Leaving my last resort, I looked up to the sky and breathed this prayer, "God, this is too big for us, so I give it to You. You are the only One who can help us now."

The day my husband had to face the bankers, I sat on the couch and listened to him explain our dilemma. All he had to offer them was a mere $3,000 that we had just received as an inheritance. We had no other options so we prayed together before he left. He was afraid. As he stood up to leave, suddenly he did a crazy thing. He lifted the check to the ceiling and said, "I offer this money to You, Lord. Please bless and multiply it like You did the five loaves and two fishes. We need a miracle!"

You may think this a noble act of faith, but I felt it was foolish. Because I had been raised in a very practical Christian home, I felt like my husband was being a dreamer. My common sense shut down the potency of this small act of faith.

"Okay, now I know you've lost your marbles," I said to him. "You just can't take the Scripture literally." Besides I couldn't imagine how they could take his offer of $3000 for $13,000 seriously.

But guess who was wrong? The bank did, of course, reject his offer of $3,000, but they countered with $8,000 to settle the loan. The bankers even agreed to let him pay off the $5,000 balance in five years with no interest. The problem was we could not scrape enough together for the extra monthly payment. When my husband explained the offer to his boss,

"Okay, now I know you've lost your marbles," I said to him. "You just can't take the Scripture literally."

who had been advising him, he was thrilled with the counter offer and baffled by my husband's lack of enthusiasm until Stan admitted to him we were barely covering basic expenses. But God is a creative God and was not finished working all things for good.

"Oh, that's no problem," his boss said. "I'll just raise your salary enough to cover the monthly payment with a little extra to cover the income taxes." And this from a boss who was tight as a drum. Now that was a miracle! And so in time this debt was cleared without one penny actually coming from our own pockets. "But be doers of the word, and not hearers only" (James 1:22).

When my husband found himself in trouble, he sought the Lord for help. He spontaneously prayed with an innocent heart and childlike faith a prayer that pleased God, acting on the words that Jesus had prayed 2000 years ago. We did not deserve the heavenly handout we received, but God chose to honor his prayer because he acted in faith. Stan put God's words into action in a very practical way. I can't explain what happened with us in theological terms. I simply accept the fact that when we act in faith, it pleases Him.

The Lesson:

Doing the Word of God is a powerful method for building a life foundation. When we hear the words of Jesus and act on them, even in the smallest way, we are building our lives on Him. "If you have faith the size of a mustard seed, you will say to this mountain, 'Move from here to there,' and it will move; and nothing will be impossible to you" (Matt. 17:20).

Power Principle:

How was it possible for us to settle a $13,000 debt with not one cent from our own pockets? We had been hard at work during this period of time placing our finances in alignment with the principles of the Bible. Belief in the principles about money in the Bible required obedience. Little by little, we learned how to walk closer to God and obey His commands concerning money. And with this small act of faith, my husband connected to the God of supernatural increase. Instead of good luck, it was good faith because of whom we put our faith in. Acts of faith don't have to be large to be effective. God lets us start small—with faith the size of a mustard seed.

> And with this small act of faith, my husband connected to the God of supernatural increase. Instead of good luck, it was good faith.

Begin by praying for God's will to be done. Don't be afraid to ask for help or for blessing in specific areas of your life, and then watch God's Spirit go to work. The simple action of asking begins the faith process. Many people feel like it is presumptuous to ask God for help, especially when the troubles are of our own making. But didn't God provide clothes and food for Adam and Eve even after they had disobeyed His direct order not to eat of the fruit of the forbidden tree?

God is in the process of providing, guiding, and developing character in His kids, even when we do wrong. He does not abandon us when we get off track or make willful decisions against Him. He stands near, waiting to be invited back into our lives. It is our right and privilege to come to Him for help because He is our heavenly Father and He wants what is best for us.

Many times Christians hesitate to ask for God's supernatural intervening power because of their subconscious fear of "using God" to serve their own selfish purposes. Though most of our prayers are ego-driven, God knows and understands that. The funny thing is, He wants a relationship with us even while we are growing. He loves us not because we are perfectly formed, but because we are His, just as we love our children in spite of their self-centeredness.

We all need to be more child-like in our prayers, looking to Him for help and protection. My husband came to God with his offering in hand, reached up to the heavens, and asked for God's blessing on it. What could be more pleasing to God than that?

He does not abandon us when we get off track or make willful decisions against Him. He stands near, waiting to be invited back into our lives.

He loves us not because we are perfectly formed, but because we are His.

Chapter 12

Taking God at His Word

For it is God who is at work in you, both to will and to work for His good pleasure.

—Philippians 2:13

During this period of intense financial pressure, I was in charge of paying the bills while my husband worked two jobs. So much anxiety surrounded the reconciliation of our checkbook that I began to develop a phobia about facing the task. Making the numbers of the checkbook match the bottom line of the bank statement was always a challenge and rarely successful.

One day after spending what seemed like hours trying to discover the discrepancies between the two, I was so frustrated I began to cry. Those of you with swift mathematical brains may not appreciate the dilemma I faced each month. Our budget was so tight that even pennies could mean the difference between a bounced check and a reprieve.

> "Lord, please help me. I cannot figure this out! You said I have the mind of Christ, so let Him reconcile this checkbook."

So with emotion I prayed, "Lord, please help me. I cannot figure this out! You said I have the mind of Christ, so let Him reconcile this checkbook." I remember laying my head down on the obstreperous checkbook before I decided to try again. Going back through the statements one more time, I found the pesky problem, and you know what happened?

The numbers reconciled to the penny! "Hallelujahs!" and "Praise the Lords!" rang from my conservative Baptist lips to rival the best of them. I understood from the bottom of my heart (and checkbook register!) what it felt like to praise the Lord. From that point on, I never even picked up a pencil or went near the monthly statements without first voicing this prayer: "Lord, I thank You that You have given me the mind of Christ. Let His mind be active in me and help me reconcile this checkbook. In Jesus' name, amen."

As a result, every time I reconciled the statement to the penny I jumped for joy and encircled that precious dollar amount, adding PTL! in red pencil. I followed this routine faithfully for months on end until I got cocky and tried without praying first, always with the same results—no perfect calculations. In this way the Lord personally tutored me in the ways of accounting until the day came when I actually could do it on my own. But I always knew I could call on Him if I ever got in trouble. "Not only is this so, but we also rejoice in God through our Lord Jesus Christ, through whom we have now received reconciliation" (Rom. 5:11).

About this time, the Lord began to convict me concerning the tithe. I had been raised in a tithing household and knew well the benefits and blessings of giving to God first. Money had never seemed to be an issue in my childhood home, even though a preacher's salary is modest. We always seemed to have more than enough.

"Is it right to give ten percent of your income to the church when the IRS has a threatening lien on your home?"

But for the first fourteen years of our married life, we constantly struggled with financial insufficiency. God put before me a truth in His Word concerning the tithe that I had seen many times before: "'Bring the whole tithe into the storehouse, so that there may be food in My house, and test Me now in this,' says the Lord of hosts, 'if I will not open for you the windows of heaven, and pour out for you a blessing until it overflows'" (Mal. 3:10).

The problem was that though I knew this verse and had practiced it in the past, things were different now. We were not able to pay all of our bills, and we were deeply in debt. The questions around our household became, "Do you pay your tithe first or your debts?" "Is it right to give ten percent of your income to the church when the IRS has a threatening lien on your home?" Neither of us could be sure, for there seemed to be no clear answer in the Bible.

Or was there? As I began to investigate the subject, I noticed the Scriptures using the word *first* many times in conjunction with the admonition to tithe. I was struck by the tithe being called "the first fruits," so I deduced, more from conviction than logic, that we needed to pay our tithe first before we payed our obligations.

My husband had always been a generous giver to the church whenever he received any commissions, but we had not developed the discipline of paying the tithe. So after a long season of suffering financially, I committed to the Lord to tithe first before paying any other bills, and I faithfully did so for several pay periods. Everything went smoothly. One month I realized I had forgotten to pay our tithe and we were already out of money. I fell to my knees and asked God to forgive me; my heart wanted to obey but my mind had slipped.

"Lord, You know my heart. I really wanted to tithe. Please forgive me. Help me be faithful," I asked.

I was upset because each month I tithed first we had enough money for bills and food and I began to feel secure. I recognized that the order that had come into our finances was directly linked to putting God first, and I feared what might happen. But even more than that, the Lord had proven Himself so faithful to us that I didn't want to disappoint Him.

That night when I went to collect the checks my piano students laid on my piano, there was only one. Someone had decided to pay for lessons and piano books in advance. My heart skipped a beat and tears sprang to my eyes as I realized the amount of the check was the exact amount of the tithe we owed—to the penny!

My heart understood before my mind could grasp it—that God had done another incalculable favor for me. He provided "seed to the sower." "Now He who supplies seed to the sower and bread for food, will supply and multiply your seed for sowing and increase the harvest of your righteousness" (2 Cor. 9:8,10).

You can be sure I did not "pass go" with that check but took it the very next day to my church's office and signed it over to "the storehouse." That was not my money, it was His. We don't often see immediate results of our obedience, but we must trust that our obedience is paving the way to the blessings God promises in His Word.

The Lesson:

God is a God of specifics. If He says He'll do a thing, He will, down to the last penny. Our part of the equation is to factor in belief and obedience, two sides of the same coin. "Therefore, everyone who hears these words of Mine, and acts upon them, may be compared to a wise man, who built his house upon the rock" (Matt. 7:24).

Power Principle:

A wise man builds his life on the teachings of Christ. You can say you have faith in God, but until you "put your money where your mouth is," you really can't make that assertion. Actions speak louder than words. Many people have a problem with the church preaching about the tithe, but the message comes straight out of the Word of God in Malachi. This is the only place in the Bible where God invites His people to test Him. The state of your finances is important to God. More scriptures in the Bible relate to money and provision than to faith and love. If you can't trust God with your money, you can't really trust Him in any other way.

If you can't trust God with your money, you can't really trust Him in any other way.

The patriarchs of the Old Testament gave ten percent of all they owned to God. In this way, they connected to the covenant blessings God had promised His people, and they were recorded as being prosperous. When His people turned away from God, invariably they quit giving their tithe to Him. When they lost their connection to Him, they floundered. "You are cursed with a curse, for you are robbing Me" (Mal. 3:9). When they put their faith in Him as their God, they prospered. "All the nations will call you blessed, for you shall be called a delightful land" (Mal. 3:12).

The promise in Malachi is a remarkable one, as true for us today as it was then. He wants to pour out a blessing on you until it overflows. Furthermore, in Malachi 3:11, He promises to "rebuke the devourer for you" so that it may not destroy the fruits your labor. What could be better than that? To have God prosper you and protect your interest is the best insurance you could have. This is a promise you should act on.

To have God prosper you and protect your interest is the best insurance you could have. This is a promise you should act on.

After you hear His voice through His Word, the challenge of obedience arrives on the doorstep. In acting on His Word, I discovered that not only was I building my house upon the rock, I was also walking in one of the greatest adventures of life, one filled with great rewards. Don't just take my word on it, take His.

ABCs of WordSpeak
C—Confession

But having the same spirit of faith, according to what is written,
"I BELIEVED, THEREFORE I SPOKE," we also believe,
therefore we also speak.

—2 Corinthians 4:13

Chapter 13

Confess with Your Mouth

So that we may know the things freely given to us by God, which things
we also speak, not in words taught by human wisdom,
but in those taught by the Spirit, combining spiritual thoughts
with spiritual words.

—1 Corinthians 2:13

God has freely given us His Word in which He reveals His promises to those who obey. When we pray for God's promises to come true in our lives, we are simply taking God up on His offer and bringing our circumstances to His attention. When the Spirit gives us thoughts based on the Scriptures, we must learn to act on them by combining them with spiritual words, both in our prayers and in our conversation. We must make sure the confessions of our mouths agree with the Word of God. I experienced the power of confession long before I understood the principle.

Without fully realizing what was happening in my early life, one lesson after another imparted this truth of taking God at His Word, believing it in my heart, and confessing the truth with my mouth. I wish I had known the curriculum from the outset, for perhaps it would not have taken so long to learn these lessons. But I did not. I am thankful for a faith-filled husband, who even without a Christian upbringing was more likely to take God at His Word than I, a born-again Christian since the age of five, who was raised in the church.

Because the benefits and beauty of the Christian life were so new to him, he was hungry to learn the messages of the Scriptures. In his search to understand the Bible, Stan was introduced to the organization called CBMC—now called Connecting Businessmen to Christ—whose mission was to evangelize and disciple men in the marketplace. Their predominant means of conveying the gospel and its teaching was life on life. Their primary disciplines were Scripture memorization and accountability. Dave Rathkamp, Metro Director for the Houston area, spent untold hours coaching Stan in the basics of the Christian life, and through him Stan learned how to be a Christian husband, father, and businessman. For the first time in his life, Stan felt total acceptance by another man.

The men of CBMC became God's hands and feet to share the love of God with my husband. Through small group Bible studies, Scripture memorization, and a great deal of spiritual parenting, Stan grew by leaps and bounds in his faith. It is no wonder a passion ignited in him to share these messages with other men who are as much in the dark as he had been. Stan now serves as a CBMC Metro Director for the greater St. Louis area of Missouri and Illinois.

> The men of CBMC became God's hands and feet to share the love of God with my husband.

One of the hallmark verses within the CBMC organization is: "But seek first His kingdom and His righteousness; and all these things shall be added to you" (Matt. 6:33).

This verse assured the men that if they were faithful to seek Him, God would provide, thus lifting the burden of the sole provider from their shoulders. They were trained to be a disciple of Christ first and a businessman second. Stan became confident that his first priority in life was winning and discipling men, becoming less obsessed with acquiring the things we needed to live. Whenever I grew concerned with the "things" of life, he quoted this verse to me. Like many others, when struggling to put something together, I am impatient and fail to read the directions. I knew the verse by memory, but my husband knew the verse by heart. Soon we would both know it by experience.

About this time Stan was fired from his job because of someone else's mistake, and he did not even defend himself. Instead of being outraged, we both felt God had released him from a job with no future for him and was moving him into his divine destiny. Sounds elevated, but that is exactly what happened. "God means this for our good," I repeated to myself to bolster my spirits.

My husband now had more time to disciple men, when before he was tied to a desk. However, as time went on, I became more concerned about where the next paycheck would come from. I was certain this divine destiny would include a normal paying job.

"Seek first the kingdom of heaven and all these things will be added to you," Stan would declare with maddening consistency. Frankly, that concept frightened me because I thought it might give my husband license to shirk his responsibility.

"You can't take that literally," I invariably responded. "You have to find a job!" As a wife and mother of three young children, I knew someone had to be practical.

But as God would have it, when Stan was busy discipling men in the restaurants around town, a former business acquaintance "happened by" and they renewed their business together. Money came in fairly consistently, but I wanted the security of a full-time job. We still had great debts to pay. One day as I was complaining to my husband about the need for financial security, he simply asked me how much I needed at the moment.

Brazenly and without much thought, I picked an exorbitant amount. "A thousand dollars," I said.

"Okay," he answered quietly. "I'll ask my Father for it."

"We agreed not to do that again," I protested, thinking he was talking about borrowing money from his dad. But of course, he wasn't suggesting that at all.

"I mean I'll ask my heavenly Father."

> In my spiritual self-righteousness and religious mind-set, I later told God, "You can't keep doing that or he will never find a job!"

You can imagine my surprise when he came home later that week with several hundred-dollar bills in a plain white envelope. I was horrified, thinking he had robbed a bank. He only responded with assurance and suggested I count the bills, which of course, added up to the amount requested.

In my spiritual self-righteousness and religious mind-set, I later told God, "You can't keep doing that or he will never find a job!" Thank goodness God was patient with me, for He had already found an occupation for Stan, one that would require complete reliance on Him for his support. But first, He had to teach me how to "consider the lilies of the field, how they toil not, neither do they spin." God wanted me to know that He would take care of me as well.

I was in the process of learning how not to be anxious for my life, as to what I would eat or what I would wear. It was my turn to learn the lessons of the Scriptures that my husband knew so well. In the end, he was right and I was wrong. God would provide for us all we needed for life and for godliness. He would find the work my husband was to do. We simply had to remember to look to Him first. "If you then, being evil, know how to give good gifts to your children, how much more shall your Father who is in heaven give what is good to those who ask Him" (Matt. 7:11).

The Bible makes it clear that we can ask anything of Him. There are so few references forbidding us to ask for certain things, you would be hard pressed to find them.

I often hear the statement, "I would never ask God for money or material blessing. That would be selfish!" The statement itself smacks of pride and self-reliance. The Bible makes it clear that we can ask anything of Him. There are so few references forbidding us to ask for certain things, you would be hard pressed to find them. On the other hand, numerous references tell of the open door policy God holds in regard to His children. He loves to give good gifts to His children who walk uprightly. From the beginning of the garden of Eden, God instructed man to work, but He would provide.

The Lesson:

When God answers your prayers based upon His promises, no favoritism is involved. He is simply keeping His Word. "God is not a man, that He should lie . . . Has He said, and will He not do it? Or has He spoken, and will He not make it good?" (Num. 23:19).

Power Principle:

When Stan and I first began to talk about the principle of seeking first God's kingdom and ways, we were subconsciously making decisions as to whether or not we would believe God. My husband chose to make meeting with other men a priority because God was calling him into full-time ministry. But first we both had to know in our hearts that God would indeed take care of our physical needs. God proved Himself faithful every time we trusted in His Word and believed Him.

When we began to confess that God's Word was true to one another and to those we were influencing, another dimension of faith was added. We told others that His Word is true and reliable. We are not responsible for making God's Word trustworthy. We are only responsible for sharing it with others.

God's words are like spiritual vitamins. As His Word abides in us, it produces internal changes. As we speak His Word, we actively cooperate with His plan.

> God's words are like spiritual vitamins. As His Word abides in us, it produces internal changes. As we speak His Word, we actively cooperate with His plan.

We become collaborators in bringing His purposes to pass by speaking in faith the words of His promise. I have come to believe that the Holy Spirit is attentive to the words of God being spoken. The Lord God explained it to His young prophet, Jeremiah, like this: "You have seen well, for I am watching over my word to perform it" (Jer. 1:12).

Even now, God is watching over His Word. When we take in His Word and believe it, faith grows. When we speak it out, God's Spirit takes over. Many scriptures tell us of God's faithfulness to back up His promises. In other words, He keeps His Word. You become the bearer of His favor because you choose to believe and speak His promises. It is that simple.

Chapter 14

Confession of Agreement

Again I say unto you, that if two of you shall agree on earth as touching any thing that they shall ask, it shall be done for them of my Father which is in heaven.

—Matthew 18:19 (KJV)

W e just need to touch and agree." I had often heard my mother's friend, an African-American Baptist preacher's wife, use this phrase when we were facing some problem that needed prayer. Though I did not know the expression was Scripturally based, I understood that what we were doing was coming together in agreement over some stubborn issue in someone's life, determined to pray it through. Years later, my friend and I practiced this very principle without realizing it.

Mary Ellen and I often called each other and threw out the question, "Does God *really* provide?" With her five children and my three (my fourth coming later), we often encouraged each other when the problem of feeding and clothing our kids loomed large. We each had experienced God's faithfulness, but when times got tough our emotions wavered.

During one particularly stubborn period of distress, we sat at her kitchen table, encouraging each other over coffee and prayer. I had brought a few groceries for her and she protested, knowing we weren't in much better shape. "Never you mind," I said. "You know my Father owns the cattle on a thousand hills" (Ps. 50:10), and then we giggled like friends sharing a secret.

We often spoke these words to each other, to remind ourselves that we belonged to a loving Father in heaven who happened to be very rich. "Don't forget your daughters," we often said jokingly. We were young and didn't know what else to do to muster the courage to face each day.

In the driveway that day, we signed off saying, "Remember, our Father owns the cattle on a thousand hills!" While we stood talking, a nice man in a uniform walked up to us, interrupting our pep talk.

"Never you mind," I said. "You know my Father owns the cattle on a thousand hills," and then we giggled like friends sharing a secret.

"Excuse me, ma'ams. I was supposed to be delivering an order of meat to the lady across the street, but she's not home, and I sure don't want to go back to San Antonio with it in my truck, so I was wondering if either of you would want to take this order of a side of beef." He didn't stop to take a breath but continued explaining that this was top quality steak and various cuts of beef, freshly butchered and packaged, and he said he would give us a discounted price.

We looked at him without answering, not daring to look at each other. Of course, we were thinking, *Steaks? Are you kidding me? We're doing good to feed our kids macaroni and cheese with a bit of hamburger!* But he wasn't giving up.

"These are nice cuts," he continued, "hamburger, roasts, steaks, wrapped in the best quality paper that will last in the freezer for a whole year."

Finally, one of us smothered our laughter long enough to say, "Sorry, we can't really afford it at this time."

"But you don't understand," he said desperately. "I can't go back to my boss with this load of beef. I tell you what I'm going to do. I'll give it to you for half-price. You can't say no to that."

As he continued to talk about the quality of meat and the great deal, he got the big idea that we could split the order. We looked at each other, did a little fast calculating in our heads, and with a bit of faith agreed to the deal. The offer that started out over $300, ended up costing us $75 apiece for an amount of meat that would last us a long time. We each nervously wrote a check for the amount while the young man divided it up and helped us put it in her freezer and the back end of my car.

When we finally parted ways, we were hysterical with laughter because we had just shared an experience that now included the Lord. Through tears of laughter and joy, we went away saying, "Not only does our Father own the cattle on a thousand hills, He has it butchered, wrapped, and delivered to our door!" "And my God will supply all your needs according to His riches in glory in Christ Jesus" (Phil. 4:19).

Unwittingly, Mary Ellen and I had been speaking God's Word over our circumstances for a while. All we knew was that each time we did we felt better. Neither of us expected God to provide in such an extravagant way. In fact, we struggled to hold any expectation of answered prayer at this early point in our lives, and yet, God graciously answered. But now I know and understand that wherever God's Word is spoken in prayer and faith, He delivers!

> But now I know and understand that wherever God's Word is spoken in prayer and faith, He delivers!

The Lesson:

Whenever two people speak God's Word in agreement and in faith, God moves because He is watching over His word to perform it. "For where two or three have gathered in My name, there I am in the midst of them" (Matt. 18:20).

Power Principle:

When two or more agree as touching anything on earth, power is released between them. Your spirit touches another and forms a more powerful belief system. Not only that, the Bible tells us that Jesus promises to be there with you, creating a formidable alliance. When you talk about the things of the Lord, and when you invoke the name of Jesus, the powerful Holy Spirit arrives and pays attention to what is being said. What an amazing concept that God entrusts us with the name of Jesus and with His word.

> When you talk about the things of the Lord, and when you invoke the name of Jesus, the powerful Holy Spirit arrives and pays attention to what is being said.

Confession is an important tool in the life of a believer, for your mouth confesses what the heart believes. When you tell someone else that you believe some concept in God's Word to be true, his or her faith is challenged and encouraged. The Bible tells us to "speak to one another with psalms, hymns, and spiritual songs" (Eph. 5:19). In doing so we are building up one another in the faith. God stands behind His Word, and our confession puts His Word out into the open. Then He moves to back up His Word.

> God stands behind His Word, and our confession puts His Word out into the open. Then He moves to back up His Word.

In speaking God's Word into our existence, we become like one of His prophets of old. "Jesus is my Lord" is one type of confession. "His Word is true" is another. When circumstances overwhelm you, when fear and anxiety threaten to overturn your emotional boat, you are more likely to make mistakes. That is when confession of God's Word is an effective tool. I remember my grandmother quoting one of her favorite verses: "I have been young, and now am old, yet I have not seen the righteous forsaken or his children begging for bread" (Ps. 37:25).

I clearly remember the words spoken in her southern drawl, usually punctuated after a pause with a "honey!" as if to say "amen" at the end. She lived through the Depression and had experienced the worries of life. Something about the way she quoted it lent authority and certainty. I never knew another person who lived life with such lack of anxiety as my Mamaw Bryan. Though I would not fully understand her confession until years later, I realize now the seeds of faith were planted deep within me years before at my grandmother's table.

Chapter 15

Confession of Praise

You shall remember all the way which the Lord your God has led you in the wilderness these forty years, that He might humble you, testing you, to know what was in your heart whether you would keep His commandments or not.

—Deuteronomy 8:2

On the occasion of my husband's fortieth birthday, I surprised him with a party. I decorated with a large banner, saying: "You shall remember all the way which the Lord your God has led you in the wilderness these forty years."

We were in our tenth year of the terrible struggle to stay afloat financially. Although I chose the message for a little lighthearted fun, deep inside I hoped that the magic number "40" would bring a change for us. In the early years, our life was like that of the children of Israel stumbling around in the desert just outside the Promised Land. God provided the miracles of manna, water, and occasionally quail, but it was definitely inconsistent with the abundant life Jesus promised in John 10:10.

In the wilderness, I was being trained in the particulars of prayer that would help me gain my promised land. Looking back, it is easy to see

When my prayers were tied to the Scriptures, I prospered. When tied to my flesh, I floundered. However, when my heart and the confessions of my mouth agreed with the promises of God, I soared!

that when my prayers were tied to the Scriptures, I prospered. When tied to my flesh, I floundered. However, when my heart and the confessions of my mouth agreed with the promises of God, I soared!

But also like the children of Israel, before the truth could be absorbed, a bit of "unlearning" had to happen. We also had to be retrained in our thinking before we could handle the blessings of our promised land. Fortunately, our wilderness lasted only fourteen years instead of forty, but it was a long fourteen years.

During the first decade of the struggle, I learned a few things about trusting God. My heart operated in faith for one period of time, only to reset into worry mode the next. Little did I know that the verse I had displayed so boldly on that banner was a preview of coming attractions.

One of the most frightening times of our life came when we had to face the IRS problem we had been avoiding. Stan had not paid our income taxes for two years because of the rapid succession of crises in our lives. He had chosen to pay his secretary's salary, our son's ongoing medical bills, and house payments first. Uncle Sam always got put off until the next big deal came through. When the banks called our loans and closed the line of credit we depended on to live, we both had to put our heads together to pull out of the dive.

"Did you hear that, God?" I said as I left the credit counselor's office. "No one can help us again. It looks like You're it."

I went to a financial credit counselor for help, but the counselor simply shook his head and said he couldn't help us. Unless we could find more income there was nothing he could do. I had been here before and I was not going to allow myself to slide down that hole of thinking nothing could be done—again.

"Did you hear that, God?" I said as I left the credit counselor's office. "No one can help us again. It looks like You're it."

I won't lie and say I was bouncing along with faith-filled steps and an unconcerned heart. The IRS had proven that they had the right to take all that belonged to us. My husband had finally filed income taxes by the third year and the tense negotiations had begun. We would have to pay back all the income taxes from the year before the crash, and they settled on a monthly payment of $600 based on Stan's current employment of two part-time jobs.

Lumping two years together, the $8,000 we owed somehow ballooned to $25,000 once all the current taxes, interest, and penalties were added. It was daunting, to say the least.

On a Friday, Stan settled the payment schedule, the menacing Uncle Sam was appeased, and we left home to celebrate the long Labor Day weekend, breathing a sigh of relief. But at the beginning of the next work week our reprieve ended and a new challenge presented itself. A pink slip was waiting for Stan for the part-time job that supplied more than fifty percent of our income. In those days, it seemed that a weekend of peace was all we were afforded.

Uncle Sam had already paid a visit to our home, taking photos of the house and all its contents. When the man began to take pictures of an antique piece belonging to my precious grandmother, I mildly explained that they would be excluded because they belonged to my grandparents.

"You don't understand," he said coldly. "It all belongs to us." With the bank and the IRS liens on our house, it seemed as if everyone owned us. But only if we defaulted on our monthly IRS payment. With Stan's layoff, the choice each month would have to be the house payment or the IRS. Believe it or not, I was not crushed at this point. I was not hopeful either. I had finally resigned myself to the fact that we would probably lose our house, and that was vaguely okay with me. Our home had escaped foreclosure more than once in the past decade. Like a cancer patient who had taken one too many beatings of chemo, I just wanted to lay the burden down.

Like a cancer patient who had taken one too many beatings of chemo, I just wanted to lay the burden down.

After hearing the bad news, my father called and offered to pay our house note for as long as we needed. "I won't let you lose your house," he said compassionately.

"Thanks, Dad," I said, truly grateful. "I appreciate your offer, but this is God's house, and if He wants us to keep it, then He is going to have to pay for it because I'm tired of fighting for it."

So, rejecting his gracious gift, I hung up the phone and went about waiting for the axe to fall. But an odd thing happened. The Lord heard my confession. The first month the payments came due, our friend Suzan Shafi, came by carrying a plain white envelope full of hundred dollar bills. She had spent many Sundays around our table, and we had walked with her through a threatening divorce. We had helped her come to know the Lord, and she was like family to us.

"Please accept this as a gift to express my gratitude for all you and Stan have done for me," she pleaded. After much convincing I finally took the money and counted the bills. There it was again, the familiar plain white envelope filled with $1000 that my Father in heaven had provided once before. It felt like a stay of execution.

By the time the payments came due the next month, an insurance refund check came in, covering the amount of both notes. And the next month? I honestly do not remember, but we never missed another payment because we remained in the house until we sold it years later. We settled into a comfortable pattern of watching God provide, making sure His children never went begging.

But the story does not end there. For years later the story made a full circle, like those wanderers in the desert. After the fortieth birthday party, Stan called to inform me that we were being audited, and the years in question were five years before.

"Well, praise the Lord!" was my spontaneous response.

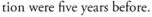

Thinking I had lost my mind, my husband replied, "Did you hear me? We are being audited! Do you know what an audit is? You don't praise the Lord for an audit!"

> "Did you hear me? We are being audited! Do you know what an audit is? You don't praise the Lord for an audit!"

Perhaps my naïveté prevented me from understanding the whole picture, but I could not help but believe that God meant this for our good. Mind you, during this time we nearly went bankrupt with business failures and medical bills. And then there was the challenge of coming up with all those pieces of paper called "receipts" from five years before.

When we arrived at the IRS with our little box of proofs, our auditor looked at us in complete dismay. "Where's your accountant . . . your lawyer?" he pleaded more than asked.

My husband responded, "I just brought my wife," to which the auditor simply rolled his eyes and in a tone fearing the worst, said: "Well then, come on in."

Walking in feeling doomed, I breathed a prayer to the only Advocate going in with us. We felt like two kids entering the principal's office awaiting our punishment. Two main questions needed to be satisfied. Why had we failed to pay income taxes for two years, and could we prove the sum of money given to the church? After several hours in the hot seat, the auditor began to have compassion on us as he reviewed our situation. At one point the tables turned and he began to help us, even finding some exemptions we had overlooked. I walked out feeling like "Mr. Smith" was our good friend in the government.

A huge rift was healed in our marriage as a result of the audit, as well as gaining a plan for getting out of debt. Seeing the tightrope my husband had been walking all those years, to pay medical bills or the government, I was able to forgive him for the financial mess we were in. We felt the heavy load we had borne for years lift off our backs and even came out with a few tax credits.

Forced by the process of the audit, we remembered the road that brought us to this point. The end result was we learned what to do and what not to do about managing money in times of crisis. We also could look back and remember how God had provided and supported us. We still had to pay the back taxes, and that took quite a while, but I am here to testify that God causes even audits to work for your good. "No discipline seems pleasant at the time, but painful. Later on, however, it produces a harvest of righteousness and peace for those who have been trained by it" (Heb. 12:11).

God disciplined us in the ways of money because we needed it and because we are His children. We repented for going ahead of God in our financial choices and we purposed never to get in that shape again. We made the course corrections that would build our character, hoping against all hope to avoid financial ruin. We learned that even when mired in the consequences of our own poor choices, God still provides, just like He did for his first two kids, Adam and Eve.

We learned that even when mired in the consequences of our own poor choices, God still provides, just like He did for his first two kids, Adam and Eve.

The Lesson:

God provides for His children even when they make mistakes. Our confession must be one of thankfulness in trials, for He disciplines those He loves. "Consider it pure joy, my brothers, whenever you face trials of many kinds, because you know that the testing of your faith develops perseverance. Perseverance must finish its work so that you may be mature and complete" (James 1:2–4).

Power Principle:

We all have to go through the wilderness at one time or another if we are to grow to maturity. Even Jesus was led by the Holy Spirit into the wilderness for a time of testing (Luke 4:1). For forty days He was tempted by the devil to disbelieve God and disobey His Word. Jesus responded each time by quoting the Word of God.

We are to follow this same pattern during times of tribulation. Jesus didn't defend Himself or assert His position. He simply quoted God's Word, and eventually the devil gave up and left Him alone for awhile. God may deliver us out of a problem, but oftentimes our prayers are answered as we walk through the valley of the shadow of death. His rod of discipline and His staff of comfort promise to guide us all the way through (Ps. 23:4).

Believing God and confessing His Word throughout the trials steadies our nerves and guides our thoughts. However, as the trial continues, perseverance in trusting Him and confessing His Word bring about endurance and proven character. God needs mature Christians to run His administration. Too many of us fall apart when times get tough. We need to grow up and become strong and unwavering. When trials grow longer, we grow stronger, if we continue to stand on God's Word.

> God needs mature Christians to run His administration. Too many of us fall apart when times get tough. We need to grow up.

The lesson we must learn is to continue to trust God in the dark. He is as good in the dark as He is in the light. Our confession must be "Praise the Lord!" in the face of desperate circumstances. As you pray for relief, continue to thank Him for His provision—even before it comes. What you do during the wilderness experience will lengthen or shorten the time spent there. When you confess with your mouth that what God says is true, not only are you building your faith, but you are also planting seeds of faith. Not only do you pass the test, but you reap a harvest as well.

The Scriptures promise God's support when we honor Him, live for Him, and act for Him. Our part is to believe God's promises, but belief without confession is only half the solution. It is like running a race without crossing the finish line. Speaking words of faith not only encourages us, it changes the atmosphere around us. The wilderness experience should have a beginning and an end. We are not meant to live and die in the wilderness. Unless, of course, we fit the description of those children of Israel who refused to believe and act on God's leading. We must go all the way with our faith. Ask, believe, confess, act. That is the pathway out of the wilderness.

> Speaking words of faith not only encourages us, it changes the atmosphere around us.

Chapter 16

Confession of Obedience

*You will drink from the brook, and I have ordered the ravens to feed
you there. So he did what the LORD had told him. The ravens brought
him bread and meat in the morning and bread and meat in the
evening, and he drank from the brook.*

—1 Kings 17:4–6

Our Bible teacher at the latest CBMC family camp, Major Ian Thomas, taught a beautiful picture of obedience from 1 Kings 17, when Elijah first came on the scene. Each time the word of the Lord came to Elijah asking him to do something, Elijah faithfully "went and did according to the word of the Lord." God sent Elijah to a brook in the middle of nowhere where He commanded the ravens to bring him food. Elijah had pronounced a terrible three-year famine on the land as God's judgment on His people.

When the brook dried up, God sent Elijah to a widow, who like many others, was struggling to feed her son. When Elijah came to her, he asked her for some bread and water, which she would be hard-pressed to supply. She explained that she only had a handful of flour and a little oil left in the jar and was planning to prepare it for herself and her son so that they could "eat it and die."

Then Elijah did a remarkable thing. He asked her to feed him first, and if she did, he promised that her jar of oil and barrel of flour would never be empty until the Lord sent rain on the face of the earth. So she "went and did according to the word of Elijah" and sure enough she never ran out of food, according to the word of the Lord which Elijah had pronounced.

Confession of Obedience

Throughout his discourse on the power of an obedient life, Major Thomas threaded his famous motto: "If you're told what to do (by God) and do as you're told, even the ravens will feed you." Throughout the week the partici-

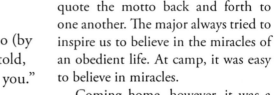

pants at the camp had fun trying to quote the motto back and forth to one another. The major always tried to inspire us to believe in the miracles of an obedient life. At camp, it was easy to believe in miracles.

> "If you're told what to do (by God) and do as you're told, even the ravens will feed you."

Coming home, however, it was a challenge to carry forth the things we'd learned at camp. Since our coffers were thin much of the time, Stan and I were greatly impacted by this teaching. When the strain of finances continued, my husband, the consummate encourager, quoted this motto to me, "If you're told what to do and do as you're told, even the ravens will feed you" and, he would add, "I'm an obedient sucker!" He was doing all he could to support his family, but the pantry shelves were depleted.

I, the consummate "stuffer," had stopped complaining about how low our food supply was. One night everything came to a screeching halt. Our Sunday school class was having its dessert party at our house, which meant I supplied the house and they, the goodies. I literally had nothing to feed the kids that night, except the snacks that were coming.

Not long before the guests were to arrive, Stan came home, and opening the refrigerator, noticed it was decidedly empty. "Whatcha feeding the kids?" he asked casually.

> "Whatcha feeding the kids?" he asked casually.
> "Nothing," I replied, as he proceeded to the pantry to find it truly bare.

"Nothing," I replied, as he proceeded to the pantry to find it truly bare. Panic rose in his voice and face as he realized the situation.

"Why aren't there any groceries?" he said, going back to the freezer, knowing full well the money had run out. "I'll rob a bank if I have to!"

"Let them eat cake." I replied with very little tongue-in-cheek. Then I quickly assured him that the kids could eat the cheese and crackers and fruits that were coming before I let them eat the cake. Food was on its way.

Before you judge me harshly, know this. I had been trying to tell my husband for awhile of our impending shortage, but not only was he distracted, he had heard it all before. His head was down, focused on work. Besides, we had been invited to a CBMC luncheon the next day and I knew we would be okay for one more day. And we did have at least $25 left in our checking account. Sure enough, before the night was over, plenty of snacks and desserts showed up at our table with enough left over for Sunday breakfast.

Sitting in church always feels safe, so we went about our Sunday morning routine as usual. When the offering plate at church came around, Stan took out the checkbook and looked questioningly at me. I knew what he was about to do, and it was okay with me. He intended to give literally the last of our barrel. I felt much like the widow from the Elijah story—what difference would it make anyway? So breathing a prayer, my husband laid his offering of twenty-six dollars and fifty cents in the plate.

> He intended to give literally the last of our barrel. I felt much like the widow from the Elijah story—what difference would it make anyway?

Looking back, I realize how depressed I truly was during this time period. I can't say I was joyful about giving "the last of our barrel." I was just numb. At home while changing clothes for our lunch engagement, Stan found a quarter in his shorts and pulled it out, saying, "Look, Laura, it's already started." Scouring the car for change for the toll booth, he came back excited, with four more quarters in his hand.

"It's already multiplied 400 percent!" he exclaimed. "If you do what you're told . . ."

"I know," I interrupted, "even the ravens will feed you." He was having much too much fun for our dire circumstances. But his attitude, no matter how real or contrived, was contagious. Deciding not to take the toll, he laid the $1.25 in change on top of our sideboard so it could "mate and multiply while we were gone," so he said.

We all hopped in the car and began the long drive to our destination, where we would be fed in return for serving on a family camp committee. Following the directions we were given, we continued until we came to a stop light.

"What street do we turn on?" Stan asked, interrupting my daze. I looked down at the directions in my hand and up at the large green sign hanging over the cross street and down at the directions again. I froze. "Well?" Stan said, impatiently, "Do I turn here or not?" It took a second or two for me to answer.

"Yes, turn right here." And then I asked, "Is this some kind of joke?" But there it was, the biggest, greenest street sign I had ever seen displaying the name "RAVENSWAY" in capital letters. And just in case we missed the point, the directions continued to guide us past Ravens Caw, Ravens Nest, Ravens Pass. You get the picture.

We arrived at our destination and I gave the kids their last minute admonitions to use their manners punctuated with the tag, "And be sure to go back for seconds!" We walked up to the door, rang the bell, and were greeted by our host who, I kid you not, had the blackest hair and a beakish nose that gave him the unmistakable appearance of a raven.

Inwardly I chuckled, *"So, these are the ravens who will feed us? Lord bless them."*

It was a wonderful day, and even though no one could know our inward fears, I felt relieved being around nice people and good food. Going home, everyone settled into the warm car for the long ride home, feeling the contentment of a full stomach. Stan's friend, Bruce Witt, had handed him a small book entitled *Let Go* by François Fénelon, and he laid it on the console between us.

"You don't know how hard it was, for me to put that money in the offering plate today. It was like taking food out of my kids' mouths."

If we let go, we'll drown, I thought as I read the title. I picked up the book and thumbed through its pages. As I did, money spilled out into my lap—$120 in cash.

"What did you do? Ask him for money?" I asked. How sad that the only emotion I felt in that instant was embarrassment. But looking at Stan I could see his answer. Tears streamed down his face as he shook his head from side to side, mouthing the word "no."

Gaining his composure he was finally able to say, "You don't know how hard it was, for me to put that money in the offering plate today. It was like taking food out of my kids' mouths."

We were at the beginning of a remarkable time of experiencing God's grace and getting to know God as Father in very personal and practical ways. The words of the motto from camp weren't simply catchy, they were true!

An alarm bell in heaven went off that morning when Stan offered God the "last of our barrel." God knew of our dilemma and moved on our behalf. It became very personal to God when we put the full weight of our trust on Him. Because my husband had planted the smallest seed in faith, God came in and took over.

By the end of the next week, Stan received a raise from his part-time employer, which was initially paid to him in the form of a check for $1,200. A week after that, we received an unexpected refund from an insurance company for double that amount. Does God have a sense of humor? Probably, but these provisions weren't a whim of God. They lined up with a law of God

An alarm bell in heaven went off that morning when Stan offered God the "last of our barrel." God knew of our dilemma and moved on our behalf.

that says the just shall live by faith, and whatever a person sows that is what he or she reaps. I thank the Lord that He prepared us for this time of famine and filled our mouth with a good word and good food. "In times of disaster they will not wither; in days of famine they will enjoy plenty" (Ps. 37:19).

The Lesson:

If you do what you're told, and you're told what to do by God, even the ravens will feed you. (Who can improve on that?) "For I am not ashamed of the gospel of Christ, for it is the power of God to salvation for everyone who believes, for in it the righteousness of God is revealed from faith to faith; as it is written, 'The just shall live by faith'" (Rom. 1:6–7).

Power Principle:

Fortunately, God had planted the seeds of faith deep within us before this particular time of famine hit. Famine comes to all of us in some way or another. It is beneficial for you to store up words of faith before the famine comes. We had been surrounded by people of faith, who believed deeply the things of God. We also had planted the Word of God into our minds and slowly but surely, with experience, our hearts began to believe. Speaking affirmations of faith based on Scripture is one way to plant seeds in dry places. You can then water your prayers by repeated confessions of faith in God's promises.

Most of us do not understand the power of the spoken word. After all, God spoke the world into existence. He didn't mold it with His hands. He spoke a word and it was done. God said and then God called it good. Once God declared it, the Spirit of God began to move over the face of the earth and cause it to come into being. "By faith we understand that the worlds were framed by the word of God, so that the things which are seen were not made of things which are visible" (Heb. 11:3).

> Most of us do not understand the power of the spoken word. After all, God spoke the world into existence. He didn't mold it with His hands.

You might protest that we are not God. But God did say that He made us in His image, did He not? Therefore, to a lesser degree we have some of the same capabilities He has. Like Him, we have the capacity to feel, to decide, to love, to create life. We have the capacity to take away life if we so choose. Therefore, why wouldn't our words be important? His were and so are ours. We decide whether to choose words of life or words of death.

The theme interwoven from the first to the last chapter of this guidebook is the power of your voice to change your future. When you hear the Word of God, come into agreement with it, and declare it over your concerns, your circumstances will line up with God's will. God has spoken it first, and you are simply coming into agreement with Him. If you use the power of your voice to agree with God, you will get lasting results: "The grass withers, the flower fades, but the word of our God stands forever" (Isa. 40:8).

Chapter 17

Confession of Healing

Is any among you sick? Let him call for the elders of the church, and let them pray over him, anointing him with oil in the name of the Lord; And the prayer offered in faith will restore the one who is sick.

—James 5:14–15a

The pulmonologist had just released my mother from her long-standing treatment for bronchiectasis and tuberculosis. They could do nothing more. We were all so saddened to hear the news for we had placed our hope in the treatments given at the lung hospital in Tyler, Texas. A long run of heavy illness had plagued her for sixteen years. No one seemed to have any faith left to pray for her healing, least of all me, who had been struggling myself with some type of chronic syndrome for seven years. That night, I prayed that God would give me some words of comfort for my parents. My family had a habit of looking to the *Daily Light* for guidance and encouragement, so I opened it to the day's reading and was struck by the bluntness of His answer. The title scripture in bold letters simply said, "The end will come."

Wow, those are not comforting words, I thought, so I skipped over to the evening's selection, which began, "Is any one of you sick? He should call the elders of the church to pray over him." Now I was confused. Was the answer to my prayer the first verse or the second one? We were a part of a church denomination that did not typically pray over the sick the way the verse in James directed. So what did this mean?

God had indeed spoken, but how was I to interpret His answer which seemed like a contradiction? I filed this away and pondered it until I could later share with my husband.

As soon as we were on our way home, I explained to Stan the timelines, the prayers, and the verses and asked his opinion. He hesitated briefly and then answered, "I think the first verse is for your mother, and the second verse is for you."

I felt a bit shocked, for we had not been talking about my condition, nor had we for a long time. It had come to be an accepted part of our lives. This sickness took me down a winding road of various and sundry illnesses that had symptoms ranging from the minor flu-like symptoms to the more serious hepatitis and pancreatitis.

> Each assault on my body left me weak and wondering if I would ever again live a normal life.

One crazy illness that took me to the emergency room in the middle of the night was "devil's grip," an inflammation of the diaphragm caused by the Coxsackie virus. Thinking I was having a heart attack, my husband called an ambulance. Each assault on my body left me weak and wondering if I would ever again live a normal life. Depression flooded in as there seemed to be no solutions.

Upon returning home, God's answer came again while I was in the health food store buying soup. My liver was inflamed, and for a week I subsisted on liquids. I ran into an old friend, who, after hearing a little of my struggle, said, "Have you ever considered calling the elders of the church to lay hands on you?"

She continued talking about the practices in her new church, but I had tuned her out to deal with my own thoughts. *Surely, this can't be what God is saying.*

A seismic shift took place in my brain. Many months before God started drawing me out of my small sphere. It all began when a bright, turquoise book in my father's home office caught my eye. Grabbing it to fill the long hours on the Greyhound bus to and from my parent's home, the book, *Healing*, by Father Francis MacNutt became my companion over the months of travel. Many questions were raised as I slowly read the pages. It was a whole new concept, that power for healing still existed today.

Simultaneously, I heard so many testimonies of healing on television when I was too ill to attend church, that it occurred to me they couldn't all be lying. I had been praying for healing on my knees beside my bed for many years, but it hadn't occurred to me to ask others pray over me. Feelings of faith began to stir deep within.

God continued His campaign as He moved Lavonia Duck, a precious counselor from our church, to offer her services at no charge. "I just want to share some things with you about what you're going through. Come see me, Laura," she had said so fervently that I couldn't refuse. As I got ready to go the morning of the appointment, I felt a strong sense that this was going to be a significant day. A sensation so strong arrested me and I prayed, "You are going to speak to me today, aren't You, Lord?"

I had been praying for healing on my knees beside my bed for many years, but it hadn't occurred to me to ask others pray over me.

Throughout the session, I remained alert as we talked through the process of grief I was going through, watching my mother slowly waste away, while balancing the rigors of our home and the stresses of our life.

I was thinking, *I know, I know, I'm sad because my mother's dying . . .* when suddenly she stopped talking and leaned her head into her hand as if to think twice.

"Laura, there's something else I want to say to you. I don't know if I should really even say this . . . but . . ."

Okay, this is it. Whatever she's about to say is directly from You, isn't it, Lord?

"Have you ever considered spiritual healing?" Her sudden shift in subject must have caused a puzzled look on my face, for she quickly explained, "What I mean is, have you ever considered the verse in James where it says, 'If any of you is sick let him call for the elders of the church'?"

I was astonished. We had not been speaking of my illness in any direct way, and here she was encouraging me to call for the elders of the church? This blew my mind. She began talking rapidly as if to explain her rash suggestion. She had heard the testimony of a lady named Dodie Osteen, who had been healed of inoperable cancer by speaking the scriptures of healing over herself and by having others lay hands on her and anoint her with oil.

I couldn't have been more shocked, listening to this former foreign missionary-turned-counselor speak of healing out of her conservative Baptist lips. As we seemed to abruptly end our session, she encouraged me to call the church in our area where Dodie and her husband had pastored to get the tape and book of her testimony. As I walked out of the counselor's office, a strange feeling of defeat came over me. Even in the face of hearing God speak, the old mind-set hung on stubbornly. I was strangely conflicted.

Two weeks later, however, God intervened again. As we left a CBMC party, a friend halted us, saying there was something she wanted to give me. Rushing to her car, she returned carrying a ziplock bag carrying the tape and book of the testimony entitled, *A Lady Named Dodie*.

After listening to the tape, I could no longer deny the constant theme. Healing power in the Word of God and the name of Jesus is available for us today. God was calling me to act on it. This lady named Dodie had experienced healing by speaking all the scriptures of healing over herself even as she bled from the effects of liver cancer. They had followed biblical protocol and called for many different elders to lay hands on her. In the end, her healing was progressive. She lived and went on to head up a significant and effective healing ministry.

"Lord, it's as if You don't even want me to find a doctor."
"I don't" came the authoritative answer.

After listening to the tape, Stan and I agreed to pray about who God would have lay hands on me, but I made Stan promise not to tell anyone. I continued to pursue the doctors, five in all, because my symptoms had gotten worse. I was having trouble lying down to sleep because of the pain in my upper abdomen. No one could pinpoint the source of the pain. I had spent numerous hours frustrated in doctor's offices. One claimed it must be depression, another suggested HIV, and another yelled at me when I questioned his diagnosis. After this particularly disheartening visit, I laid my head on the table and wept. "Lord, it's as if You don't even want me to find a doctor."

"I don't" came the authoritative answer in my mind, causing me to sit up straight. The truth was, the only answer I wanted was a good doctor and a potent pill. Whether I admitted it or not, I did not want to pursue the laying on of hands. My procrastination ended abruptly the day I came across this verse about a king named Asa: "His disease was severe, yet even in his disease he did not seek the LORD, but the physicians. So Asa slept with his fathers" (1 Chron. 16:12–13).

A sense of fear gripped me. I had better not continue ignoring God's answer. After a month of praying, I received some strange direction when my neighbor called me over to give me news of a spiritual nature. She had grown proficient in using the Ouija board and had learned to communicate with the spiritual world. To confirm her authority, she shared with me facts about our life that she could not have known.

"I know this may sound crazy to you," she told me, "but God has a commission for me. In these last days, I am to begin a healing ministry, and I am supposed to lay hands on you, and you are going to be healed." She had no idea we had been praying for just such an answer.

"Wow, that's great, but I need to pray about it first," I said and skedaddled home quite shaken and a little excited. I was not sure that she was even a Christian. I silently prayed, *"That's unusual, but if that is the way You want to go about it, You can do whatever You want with me."* But before my feet left her front porch, these words spontaneously shot out of my mouth, "Praise God from whom all blessings flow! You are the Lord, my God and I will have no other gods before You."

Fortunately, circumstances put several days and a thousand miles between me and my neighbor, for the next day, we drove to Florida for a week's vaca-tion paid for by a small inheritance from my grandmother. We were going to fulfill our dream to go to Disney World®. The kids and I had prayed nightly, and now after many years, our prayers were being answered.

I would deal with my neighbor's offer when we got back. Before we left I noticed a book, *The Beautiful Side of Evil*, lying on my kitchen counter.

If the demonic had offered me an unholy healing, then God must be offering true healing.

I didn't know how it got there. Once again, I grabbed a book for the long ride. The book was the story of a young woman who was warning others of the ability of demonic spirits to emulate healing. The book chronicled her path from psychic healer to a born-again life. It was the first time I had ever acknowledged the presence of evil spirits operating in the world.

My decision was made. If the demonic had offered me an unholy healing, then God must be offering true healing. Finally, I believed it with all my heart. When I got back, I would call the pastor of my Baptist church and ask for help, even though we had no protocol for calling the elders of the church for healing. We didn't even have elders, but since God was in charge of this from the beginning, I trusted Him to work out the details.

"I've never done this before and I don't believe that the oil has healing powers," my pastor said. "But, after hearing your story, I would be afraid not to honor your request." Then he warned me that this might not work, so I should keep on taking my medicines and staying under the doctor's care. He didn't know our COBRA insurance expired the next week, motivating me not to "chicken out."

In a matter of a few days, I was sitting in front of a dozen of the most faith-filled members of our church. The pastor opened the meeting with an interesting challenge. "The Bible says in Revelation 12:11, 'They overcame him by the blood of the Lamb and the word of their testimony.' For this reason, Laura, I'd like you to give us a word of testimony as to why we are here."

Without hesitation, I spoke the words that had been circling in my thoughts for the past two days. "God has gone to great lengths to bring me to this point, and though I do not have blind eyes to see, or crippled legs to walk, I know without a shadow of doubt that when I walk out of here, I will be healed." Why else would He have gone to so much trouble to get me to this point?

I know now that God had prepared those words for me to speak. Over the past months He had pushed and prodded, inviting me to act on His Word. The vault of tradition kept me from believing God's Word, and I am so grateful for God's patience with me.

> The vault of tradition kept me from believing God's Word, and I am so grateful for God's patience with me.

After I spoke, one by one, pastor and laymen, men and women laid hands on me. Our Baptist missionary from Africa anointed me with oil in the name of Jesus as he had done many times in the bush country. Our Chinese pastor prayed in his own language, bringing us all to tears. When we concluded, one of the men gave me a word of warning.

"The devil is going to try to make you believe you are still sick. Symptoms may hang on or return with full force. Just keep on believing and thanking God for your healing."

With that, our very first healing service was completed. My husband and I went out to eat to celebrate and then I went home and took a nap, but not before bowing beside my bed and thanking the Lord for my healing. I was exhausted.

A few days later I began having terrible nausea again, now accompanied by lightheadedness. *Goodness, the devil is doing a bang-up job of making me believe I am still sick,* I thought. Then to no one but myself I said, "I am healed by the blood of the Lamb and the word of my testimony, and I say I am healed!"

But it only got worse. If I was healed, I wouldn't feel it for another nine months, for I found out the next week that I was forty years old and pregnant with my fourth child, with a husband without a full-time job and no insurance. But that's a story for another time. "O God, You are my God, and I will ever praise You. Step by step you'll lead me, and I will follow You all of my days" (*Step by Step*, by David Beaker).

The Lesson:

When we ask, God leads, step by step. When we follow God's lead, believe His Word, and do what the Bible says, miracles happen. "For I, the Lord, am your healer" (Exod. 15:26).

Power Principle:

We have grown so comfortable with our traditional beliefs that not only do we not expect miracles, we grow uncomfortable with the suggestion of them. My story is true. God chose me as the vessel to open the door of healing in my church. We have closed the door on the power of God for so long that we have lost the expectation of God moving in powerful, unexplainable ways. But the Bible says the kingdom of God is not just a matter of talk, but of power (1 Cor. 4:20).

Speaking words of faith is a secret power that moves in the atmosphere around us, connecting us to the miracle-working power of God.

A mind-set can be like a fortress. You can change your mind-set by changing your beliefs, one at a time. You build up your faith by speaking God's Word aloud and often, so that your subconscious is transformed. Speaking words of faith is a secret power that moves in the atmosphere around us, connecting us to the miracle-working power of God.

Although it would take many months for me to enjoy the physical feeling of being healed, I knew the moment I walked out of that healing service that I had experienced a miracle. Interestingly enough, I felt nothing. My life, however, would never be the same. I could not allow myself to go back to the experience of living with a wilderness mentality. God had touched my body through the hands of believers and brought me a respite from the constant torment of fatigue and sickness.

My life was beginning to make a grand shift, out of the desert and into the promised land. In the beginning I was so impoverished that I couldn't even imagine the fruit and blessing of the kingdom of heaven. God pulled me up and out of the miry pit by handing me a process of praying that would help me fight my way out of the land of lack. First, He gave me His example by speaking the worlds into existence. Then He gave me Jesus, His living Word. Next He gave me His written Word, and on top of that He gave me a voice and told me to use it! Now that I could do.

Many trials were still to come, but my approach was different. I grew confident in God's plan and knew firsthand of the overcoming power of God through all these life experiences. By applying my faith forward heading into the storm, the wind and the waves of adversity quickly grew less fierce. No longer would God have to drag me along. I learned how to cooperate with His plan and bring His will into my life and the lives of others. Though I did not realize it then, I had grown from being someone driven and tossed by the wind to being a tree planted firmly by streams of living water who prospers in whatever she does (Ps. 1:3c).

> I learned how to cooperate with His plan and bring His will into my life and the lives of others.

As I consistently applied the ABCs I had learned in this initial stage, my prayer life grew more and more profitable. "Ask and you shall receive," "you have not because you ask not," "you ask with wrong motives"—all these verses have one thing in common. They teach us how to ask. The first lesson I had to learn in my school of prayer was to acknowledge God in everything and ask for His will to be made known. Before I was able to receive anything from the Lord, I had to learn how to ask for help.

The second lesson was the importance of belief in the prayer process. Answers to prayers don't come out of a vacuum. We must fill our hearts with habits of faith and become determined to find out the truth about God and ourselves. I had to learn the truth about what I truly believed, and whether or not my beliefs were based on the truth of God's Word or my own experiences.

And finally, I had to learn to participate with God in the answering of my prayers. Speaking God's Word became my part in actively seeding my prayers with faith. Acknowledging God's will in my mind, believing in my heart, and confessing with my mouth made the process of seeking and knocking more profitable. With the understanding of these simple ABCs, my prayers became more focused and directed.

Of course, this is not the end of my journey. In the next section I hope to draw you into this wonderful way of approaching prayer, to inspire you, even dare you to step onto that path of faith. Undoubtedly, a few may find ways to criticize my conclusions about God and attempt to place me in one theological camp or another. Please don't. I just ask you to continue to walk with me without labels. I am simply one who walks with God, and these have been my experiences. Though many types of Christian leaders have influenced me, my primary leader has been the Lord Jesus Christ, and my true guide has been the Holy Spirit.

Section Two

Get Set!

Preparing for Your Journey

Be diligent to present yourself approved to God as a workman who does not need to be ashamed, accurately handling the word of truth.

—2 Timothy 2:15

Introduction to Getting Set

Be devoted to one another . . . not lagging behind in diligence, fervent in spirt, serving the Lord; rejoicing in hope, persevering in tribulation, devoted to prayer.

—Romans 12:10, 11a, 12

N ow it is time to focus on you and the preparation for your WordSpeak journey. As this verse says, I am devoted to you for one purpose—that you can know some of the shortcuts out of the wilderness! Of course, I pray that you will ultimately be devoted to prayer and the pursuit of knowing God. The world needs consecrated Christians who are diligently and effectively serving the Lord. In order to do this, our own lives must be fearlessly moving forward to advance the kingdom of heaven, first for ourselves and then for others. We cannot do this if we don't know how to pray effectively. If we do not know the keys to the abundant life, or heaven forbid, we do not know our Commander-in-chief, we live life simply treading water. I am devoted to you for this reason, sharing with you as much as I can to inspire you to get off the bench and take part in this exciting journey.

You have read my story of coming to grips with some basic truths God has revealed in His Word about the process of effective praying. Prayer is not only an intimate relationship with the Lord, it is the work you do together to bring His will and purposes to earth. To do this effectively, you must prepare, building yourself up in the faith. Perhaps, like me, you must unlearn a few things about God and His ways. This section will help you do that.

In this section, you will discover the basics of a faith-filled prayer life. You will also begin to understand some of the reasons for your unanswered prayers. You will evaluate your capacity for faith by first dealing with doubt. Hopefully you will unearth the lies you believe about God and about yourself, and replace them with the truth.

Next you will be challenged to develop habits of faith by watching over your thought-life and your confessions. Finally, you can prepare to receive God's abundant blessings by accepting and acting on the power of the spoken word, the power of permission and the power of transformation.

The process is clear. Clean out the debris of ungodly belief systems and build a foundation of truth. Hopefully, by applying the principles in this section you will not have to spend as much time in wilderness living as I did. Although the process is simple, it is not always easy to do. Like me, you may feel very attached to your traditional belief systems. However, holding onto old habits is what kept some of the Israelites in the wilderness and out of the Promised Land. Ending a wilderness mentality is one of the goals of a mature Christian life. Keeping in mind that your mind-set determines where you live—in the wilderness or in the Promised Land, let's get prepared!

The Truth About Faith

But you, beloved, building yourselves up on your most holy faith,
praying in the Holy Spirit.

—Jude 1:20

Chapter 18

Dealing with Doubt

*But let him ask in faith without any doubting, for the one who doubts
is like the surf of the sea driven and tossed by the wind. For let not
that man expect that he will receive anything from the Lord, being a
double-minded man, unstable in all his ways.*

—James 1:6–7

What a cruel conundrum! I am unstable in all my ways because I doubt. I don't see answers to my prayers because I don't have faith. I don't have faith because I don't see answers to my prayers. I am stuck in my instability. James makes it perfectly clear why we do not receive answers to our prayers, and yet, how can we eliminate doubt when it is so entrenched?

If you can relate to my dilemma, do not despair. You can do something to eliminate doubt and build your faith. Faith, when it begins to grow, will push out doubt. But is there something we can do to help our faith grow? First, we can actively deal with doubt by putting it in the correct category. Doubt is not harmless, any more than a tumor, when left unattended. Doubt keeps our faith at bay. "Take care, brethren, that there not be in any one of you an evil, unbelieving heart that falls away from the living God" (Heb. 3:12).

> Doubt is not harmless, any
> more than a tumor, when left
> unattended.

Jesus most often chided His disciples about their unbelief. The writer of Hebrews called an unbelieving heart "evil." Therefore, as Christians we need to be careful about allowing doubt and unbelief to stay put in our lives. Though doubting is not a sin *per se*, we need to face our doubts head-on and deal with the underlying causes.

Doubts can form for many reasons. Woundedness provides the perfect habitat for doubts. Once we have been wounded, betrayed, or even disappointed, the ability to have faith as a child vanishes. Then we must work to build our faith. A timid personality also tends to be a staging ground for doubts. Doubts come when you are ignorant of God's will. In fact, ignorance is a breeding ground for doubt. Not understanding your right to ask God for help and favor and not knowing God's promises predisposes a person to unbelief. Doubts can also

Once we have been wounded, betrayed, or even disappointed, the ability to have faith as a child vanishes.

show up when you are out of sync with God. Undoubtedly (pun intended), the most common doubts rally around your ability to hear God's voice.

The most consistent question I hear is, "How can I hear the voice of God?" The first part of my answer is you will know the voice of God by its simple, authoritative tone. I have found that God is not usually wordy but simple in His conversation. He doesn't take over the conversation and dominate it like many of us do. Furthermore, He will not contradict His Word in Scripture. The best way to know God's voice is to listen to Him as you read the Bible.

The second part to my answer may alarm you at first and doesn't sound at all spiritual, but it is a worthy activity. Listen to all the competing voices in your head. No, you are not crazy, but you have thoughts and concerns that have not been addressed. These thoughts and impressions should be heard, if for no other reason than to consider whose voice they belong to. Sometimes it is the voice of the subconscious you, sometimes a parent, or a teacher, or a coach. The goal is to uncover any lies that might be lurking in your belief system.

Sometimes it is an evil voice. You will know it by its fruit. If at the end of the suggestion lies an action that would cause you to disbelieve God, then toss it out. The devil spoke in only a few recorded conversations in the Bible. One was with Eve and another was with Jesus. Both times his method of temptation was to ask a question that could cause them to doubt what God had told them. Satan is the master of creating doubt. My paraphrase of his question to Eve is, "Oh, come on. You don't really believe that God has your best interest at heart, do you?" You can read his successful campaign for yourself in Genesis 3:1–5.

The day I really blew a ministry opportunity I landed on my knees beside my bed asking God for forgiveness. During the prayer time of a Bible study I was leading, I had lost patience with one of the participants, abruptly cutting off her prayer request. The participant was being thoughtless of another participant, who was in pain. Though the reasons for my reaction were not unfounded, my response to this woman was a carnal one. I simply lost my cool. Everyone else around the table was floored. Although my co-leader certainly felt the same way I did, she would have never said it aloud. Many factors led to this unfortunate exchange, but none of them mattered because we all left feeling embarrassed and a bit wounded.

The devil spoke in only a few recorded conversations in the Bible. One was with Eve and another was with Jesus.

I had never done such a thing before. Although I apologized immediately and later in writing to each member present, the damage was done. After the ill-fated meeting, as I was on my knees confessing to the Lord, I heard these words in my head. *See, you're still not ready to be in ministry . . .* and then I shook my head to avoid hearing further words of condemnation. Remembering my commitment to listen to the voices in my head, I rewound the words and let the tape roll uncensored . . . *because you're not perfect yet.*

The statement startled me. I wasn't expecting to hear such an absurd indictment. Immediately, I identified the lie that this subconscious voice was spouting. This was not from God. This was from me. Instead of feeling condemned, I felt relieved. I would have to do some mental gymnastics to unravel what was going on in my head. I was guilty of having been unkind, and some form of amends needed to be made. On the other hand, I recognized that no matter who voiced those words, they were a lie that could keep me from ever trying to minister again, and thus could not be from the Lord.

Of course I wasn't perfect. I had made a mistake while in a ministry position, but I could still make amends, find forgiveness, and learn from it. Infallibility is not, and never will be the criterion for ministry. But my subconscious mind (or an evil voice) was trying to tell me it was so. Though

I struggled with feelings of failure, my restoration time was much shorter because I was able to face the truth about myself and the lie I had harbored.

Doubt could have set up residency in my soul, and I may never have led a group again had I not done what I am asking you to do. You must face your doubts and push against them with the truth of God's Word. First, I had to replace the lie with the truth: "If we confess our sins, He is faithful and just to forgive us our sins and to cleanse us from all unrighteousness" (1 John 1:9). And then I needed to take this statement to heart: "Therefore there is now no condemnation for those who are in Christ Jesus" (Rom. 8:1).

> You must face your doubts and push against them with the truth of God's Word.

Next, I needed to take a step of faith that forced me over the threshold of doubt. I had to show up again to use the gifts I had been given, and in doing so actively push against any doubts that God could use me in spite of my flaws. Unless you actively search out the underlying causes of your doubts about God and His Word, an unbelieving heart will grow like a cancer, keeping you from receiving all the good gifts God wants you to have.

The Lesson:

Push against your doubt by applying the Word of God to a specific situation and then take an action step based on that Word. *"My grace is sufficient for you, for my power is made perfect in weakness.' Therefore I will boast all the more gladly about my weaknesses, so that Christ's power may rest on me"* (2 Cor. 12:9 NIV).

Power Principle:

I remember now with fondness the first time I was confronted with doubt about the truth of the Word of God and my finances. I was a young single on a shoestring budget when I began to wonder about the difference between tithes and offerings. I asked God if an offering was above and beyond my tithe. Like most of us, I harbored significant doubts about God having my best interest at heart when it came

> It seemed to me that God and money did not mix.

to money. It seemed to me that God and money did not mix. Getting no immediate answer, I decided to go ahead and give the ten extra dollars to the missionary fund. I pushed against my doubts with this tiny act of faith.

Though the offering was small, the lesson was great, for the very next week, I received a check in the mail I had paid to a dentist the week before in the amount of ten dollars. There was no explanation in the envelope, but it might as well have been signed by God Himself. This was the beginning of a lifetime of proofs that I could never out-give God. Though I had heard this from my father many times before, I had to take a step of faith to push against my own doubts, for each of us must experience God's faithfulness for ourself.

You can defeat the cycle of doubt by reaching deep inside and confronting the myriad of voices that lead you to believe that God's Word is not applicable to you. By listening to your thoughts, you can take each one captive to the obedience of the Word of God. If it lines up with the Word of God, great. If not, throw it out and decide to take a stand on the truth by making a step of faith that pushes against your doubt. The first step may be as small as a ten dollar check, but I believe it will bring about huge dividends.

Chapter 19

Building Faith

And without faith it is impossible to please God, because anyone who comes to him must believe that he exists and that he rewards those who earnestly seek him.

—Hebrews 11:6 (NIV)

Any time you come to God with your prayer promises in hand, you please God. You must respond to God's offers by taking Him at His Word. When you know the truth but do not take it personally you cannot please God. Truth is not effective for you if it's lying in some dusty coffee table Bible. Truth is only effective when applied. You must participate in the truth for it to set you free. Therefore, you are responsible for acquiring the truth, believing it, and acting on it. You supply the dynamic ingredient required in all spiritual transactions— faith, the belief or confidence that God will move on your behalf. Faith is the bucket that fetches your answers from the fountain of blessings.

Faith is the bucket that fetches your answers from the fountain of blessings.

Once you have applied the ASK process to your prayers, asking Him for wisdom, seeking out answers in His Word, you can then take the action steps toward answered prayer. Certainly answers to prayer have to be waited on, but in the knocking stage you are actively professing the promises of Scripture that you have discovered. And once you have dealt with the doubts you have, you can more readily bring to the prayer process the critical ingredient that is your part to supply—faith. By telling others that you believe in a certain scripture promise as it applies to your concerns, you are acting in faith. More than once, Jesus reminded His disciples, "It shall be done to you according to your faith" (Matt. 9:29).

After I laid aside the many elements of my doubting heart, I took the position that I would become more faith-filled as I read God's Word and prayed. I still felt a bit feeble when it came to believing that God's Word could be applied to my problems. But I was climbing out of the pit that doubt puts you in, and to do this the faith muscle had to be exercised. One day as I read through Proverbs, I discovered a curious verse that pricked my interest, "Much wealth is in the house of the righteous" (Prov. 15:6).

> But I was climbing out of the pit that doubt puts you in, and to do this the faith muscle had to be exercised.

I posted the verse on the sideboard in my kitchen where I could see it as I entered the room. We were facing the challenge of three kids in college and I needed something to bolster my faith. Each time I entered the kitchen I glanced at this verse and hoped. Occasionally I prayed for the wealth needed to pay for the tuitions. Each time the kids despaired, facing the exorbitant needs of their education, I pointed to this verse and said: "Don't you know, kids? Much wealth is in the house of the righteous."

Occasionally, they asked me for something, and if I dared say we couldn't afford it, they quoted this verse right back to me, saying in a sing-song voice, "Mom, wealth is in the house of the righteous." Of course, no one truly believed it yet, but it was at least encouraging to hear.

One day while working on a ministry project in my basement, I got an idea that could create some revenue for our household. It was more than a good idea, it was an inspiration. My heart began beating faster as I envisioned the completed project. Feeling empowered and inspired, I sailed up the steps into our kitchen and came face-to-face with this verse written on a small card attached to the sideboard. The words quite literally exploded from my mouth with complete belief.

"Lord! There really is much wealth in the house of the righteous!" I said gleefully. It was as if the project had already come into being. I had no doubt that the inspired idea was from Him. Faith had become for me in that instant a powerful substance that propelled me to pray without any doubt or wavering for the success of my project. Although I had declared the posted verse ninety-nine times, belief—beautiful and unwavering—did not come until the hundredth time. I experienced a compelling, substantive force of faith in a way I had not known before.

Not only was I inspired and assured that this was a God-given idea, but I also felt the sense of confidence I needed to take the steps to develop the idea. In addition, faith became the substance that opened many doors and kept me going through the years of hard work to bring the idea to fruition. This belief produced a faith that would carry me through the length of the project. "Now faith is the substance of things hoped for, the evidence of things not seen" (Heb. 11:1).

Faith had become for me in that instant a powerful substance that propelled me to pray without any doubt or wavering.

In time I solved the problem of belief and came to understand how to apply those critical instructions found in James, "But let him ask in faith without any doubting." Since faith is the critical ingredient, we must know how to develop faith. I would much rather have Jesus say to me, "Hold on there, girl" than hear the most frequent rebuke He spoke to His disciples, "O you of little faith, why did you doubt?" Interestingly, nowhere in the Bible is someone rebuked for having faith in God for something He deemed unsuitable.

The Lesson:

I supply the critical ingredient of faith when bringing my prayer requests to the Lord. Faith then, comes by hearing, not just reading the Word of God. "So then, faith comes by hearing, and hearing by the Word of God" (Rom. 10:17).

Power Principle:

Occasionally I hear someone say, "I just don't have the faith you do," as if there was nothing they could do about it. But the truth is you can do something about your lack of faith. You can listen to the words of God in the Bible and confess them aloud. You take the measure of faith God has given you and you build upon it, for God has allotted to each a measure of faith (Rom. 12:3).

Faith, the catalyst for moving the hand of God, comes by hearing, and hearing by the Word of God. I had heard this verse many times and yet could safely say I still had a faith problem when it came to believing the promises of God. Some might say I had a heart problem, but I loved God and wanted to believe. No, the problem was in my head. Faith does not begin as an

But the truth is you can do something about your lack of faith.

achievement of the heart but of the mind-set and will. Before I could have the faith to pray, all levels of my mind had to be transformed.

Did you know that our subconscious drives our behavior? Subconscious thoughts are not changed by merely acquiring knowledge. Our subconscious has been programmed through early life experience, which comes through touching, feeling, tasting, seeing, and hearing. Impressions, good or bad, true or false, form the belief systems housed in our subconscious minds. Transforming the belief systems of the subconscious mind takes a special kind of effort. I prayed to understand the nature of changing my innermost thoughts and I believe that God showed me one way to do so.

When we speak aloud the scriptures on the WordSpeak cards, our subconscience hears and over time, faith rises. When we hide God's Word in our hearts and minds (Ps. 119:11) we are essentially planting seeds that will take root and grow into full-blown belief. Then we will have no problem believing what God is offering. Also, science has shown that when a strong emotion accompanies an experience, the impression is lasting. When circumstances corroborate the truth and you experience joy and gratitude for answers to prayer, a new godly belief system is installed. "Until now you have asked for nothing in My name; ask and you will receive, so that your joy may be made full" (John 16:24).

Transforming the belief systems of the subconscious mind takes a special kind of effort.

Faith gives us the power to hold on until the seeds of our prayers produce the fruit. When you repeat a promise from God's Word in prayer numerous times, you are fulfilling God's instruction to "pray without ceasing." Your heart begins to beat in tandem with its message and then the words begin to take on a life of their own, growing faith in the believer. Faith then becomes the springboard to action. Faith is the substance that sees the manifestation of a prayer before it becomes a reality for we walk by faith, not by sight (2 Cor. 5:7). We are not sure of what the fruit will look like, we just plant the seed. The details of answered prayers are God's business. Our business is to believe Him for the best version of our prayer to be accomplished.

Chapter 20

Faith, a Powerful Connector

I tell you the truth, anyone who has faith in me will do what I have been doing. He will do even greater things than these.

—John 14:12

Whuen we demonstrate faith, we not only please God but we also become powerful transmitters of His supply of energy. Faith is the power chord that connects us to the divine source. When we obey Jesus' mandate to have faith in God (Mark 11:22) we are placing our faith in the hands of an almighty Being who is capable of anything. For years I sang the old hymn, "Have Faith in God," without understanding its powerful message:

> Have faith in God when your pray'rs are unanswered,
> Your earnest plea He will never forget;
> Wait on the Lord, trust His Word and be patient,
> Have faith in God, He'll answer yet.

> Have faith in God. He's on His throne,
> Have faith in God, He watches o'er His own,
> He cannot fail, He must prevail,
> Have faith in God, Have faith in God.

Now I understand that faith connects us to God and His Word connects us to His will. The Bible says if anyone has faith in Jesus, he will be able to do great things. But just how many of us expect to do great things? Our faith through the years has dwindled into simply believing for heaven and its glories. And if that is all you can believe for, that is enough. But that will not get you into the ball game here on earth, nor is it enough faith to move mountains. Many times I read the following verse and others like it in the New Testament and wondered what it meant for me, "For truly I say to you, if you have faith the size of a mustard seed, you will say to this mountain, 'Move from here to there,' and it will move; and nothing will be impossible to you" (Matt. 17:20). Just what did Jesus mean when He said we could move mountains?

> Just what did Jesus mean when He said we could move mountains?

When the challenge of finding the money to pay for our son's college tuition came around, I was ready to go. My husband and I had come to the end of our abilities to pay the next installment. We had nowhere else to turn except to borrow the money. But first we agreed to pray and ask our heavenly Father what to do. So I began to pray for God to show us where we could get the money to pay the $1200 amount. During the time dedicated to this request, I came across a verse in my daily Bible reading that said: "The wealth of the sinner is stored up for the righteous" (Prov. 13:22b).

I felt like I had won a sweepstakes! The wealth of the sinner is stored up for the righteous? Wow! Because I have been given the righteousness of Christ (Rom. 5:17), I qualified. Furthermore, remembering the verse found in Hebrews 10:30, "But my righteous one will live by faith. And if he shrinks back, I will not be pleased with him," I was poised and ready to pray this verse back to God in faith. I was determined to be a doer of the Word and not a hearer only.

> I was not in any way making demands of God; I was partnering with Him to bring this scripture to life.

With excitement and childlike faith I said to Him: "We're some of the righteous, Lord. Send some of that wealth this way." Like the airport operator who stands on the tarmac guiding the large airplanes to the gates, I moved my arms like I was holding those signal lights as if directing some of that wealth this way.

Let me veer for a moment in my story to say I would be somewhat embarrassed to tell this story if it had not had such a fun ending. I was not in any way making demands of God; I was partnering with Him to bring this scripture to life. I felt God had revealed this scripture to me for just this moment to give me direction as to how to pray. I was collaborating with Him in meeting this need. My faith in the partnership was soon confirmed.

A few days later a businessman called and asked if this was the Stanley Bower residence who used to live in Houston. He explained he wanted to develop some land and records showed that a portion of the property was deeded to my husband. Even though it had to be some kind of mistake, I gave him my husband's number anyway and anxiously waited for an explanation.

Later that night, my husband explained that before we were married, some twenty-five years ago, he had served as president of a municipal utility district. In order to serve on the MUD board he had to own property in the district, so they deeded a small piece of property to him. I was thrilled at the prospects and asked how much the man was offering for the property.

"Oh, I told him I couldn't take his money because the property wasn't really mine," my husband informed me.

"What!" I cried. "You have to take that money. I prayed for it to come our way." But being a man of intense integrity, he refused. "Gee," I complained, "I was sure God sent that money our way." But my husband wouldn't budge, choosing to disagree with my interpretation of the scripture I had prayed.

I left it at that, believing deep down that it was, indeed, too good to be true. Undaunted, I continued to pray that the wealth stored up for the righteous would come our way. Lo and behold, a few days later, the same gentleman called me again, sounding desperate.

"I need your help, Mrs. Bower. I can't move forward on this project until this matter is cleared up. We've researched the title again and your husband is the only owner we've found on this easement. You have to make him take the money."

"Just leave it to me," I responded graciously, "and I'll see what I can do." Hardly able to contain myself, I called Stan as soon as I got off the phone, explaining that he needed to do this man a favor and take his offer. And then I asked him a legitimate question, "How do you know this isn't an answer to my prayer?"

Perhaps God changed my husband's mind for he did reconsider and in a short time was holding the check for $1,500! How precious of our Father in heaven to provide enough to pay for the college installment with a little left over, just like in the parable of the loaves and fishes. "For the eyes of the LORD move to and fro throughout the earth that He may strongly support those whose heart is completely His" (2 Chron. 16:9).

We had long before surrendered our hearts to God's will and purposes for our lives. Because we had settled the lordship of our lives, our hearts were completely His. God promised us that He would "show Himself strong on behalf of those whose heart is loyal to Him" (2 Chron. 16:9 NKJV). You can be in housework or you can be in business. The Bible says that God partners with those who are loyal to Him. In fact, He is looking for people all over the earth whom He can strongly support.

The Lesson:

Each time we declare God's Word and pray for it to become a reality, we are not just speaking to the air, we are forming a powerful partnership. "*If anyone loves Me, he will keep My word; and My Father will love him, and We will come to him and make Our home with Him*" (John 14:23).

Power Principle:

You would not make an important purchase or career change without first talking it over with your partner. We should think of God in these same terms. He is your greatest companion. He walks with you when your spouse or friends cannot. Therefore, whatever is of concern to you is a concern to Him. When you think of living life in partnership with the Lord, you go to Him and talk over your decisions with Him. Perhaps you see God as distant and uninvolved. If so, you must invest the time in getting to know Him through His Son Jesus.

The precepts, principles, and promises of the Bible are true in all times and all places. Whether or not you get to be the recipient of those promises is really between you and Him. When you discover a verse in the Bible that could be applied to your life, begin to plant your mustard seed of faith, and ask God for it to become a reality. You have permission to do this because you are a child of God and there is an unbreakable bond between you and your Father in heaven.

Believing God for specifics is the ground into which we sow our faith. When you see the specific thing you have prayed for come into being, it is a faith booster. The little surprises and events that come in answer to prayer nudge you closer to God. That such a great and massive God cares about your needs, great and small, is a remarkable discovery.

The unique relationship between God and the person who is willing to partner with Him to bring God's will and purposes to this earth is not only remarkable, but significant. A Christian is God's representative on earth. As

His ambassadors (2 Cor. 5:20), we partner with Him to establish His will on earth through effective praying. When we take the Word of God and apply it to someone who is lost, injured, or discouraged, we become transmitters of His love and grace to the person we are praying for. We know God wants all men to come to Him to be saved, but unless we know

As His ambassadors, we partner with Him to establish His will on earth through effective praying.

how to bring this grace into our own lives through prayer and proclamation, we won't be effective in conveying it to others.

The Truth About God

Let him who boasts boast of this, that he understands and knows Me,
that I am the LORD who exercises lovingkindness,
justice and righteousness on earth; for I delight in these things,
declares the LORD.

—Jeremiah 9:24

Chapter 21

Approaching God

Therefore let us draw near with confidence to the throne of grace, so that we may receive mercy and find grace to help in time of need.

—Hebrews 4:16

We have been given a wholehearted invitation to approach God for help, but often we lack the confidence to run boldly to His throne. In a 2005 Gallup poll done for Baylor University's Research of Religion Department, answers revealed that over 31 percent of Americans view God as authoritarian, over 24 percent view Him as distant, and 16 percent view God as critical. Even though a majority of those polled espoused religious beliefs, over 70 percent viewed God in a negative light. How many of those do you think will confidently ask God for favor and help in time of need?

> 70 percent viewed God in a negative light. How many of those do you think will confidently ask God for favor and help in time of need?

I know from experience that when we begin to understand God's heart and ways as revealed in the Scriptures, the tendency to be timid will disappear. Knowing His agenda and His heart will help you as you present your concerns to Him. Our prayer life languishes because of lack of true knowledge of our God. But we don't have to remain ignorant of God because He has chosen to reveal Himself in His Word and in His Son. In my personal "school of prayer" I experienced God in my circumstances outside the pages of the Bible that confirmed His character described in the Bible. Each time He intervened in my life in response to my prayers, I grew in confidence. Even if I did not always know His will, I knew Him. Thus my confidence in approaching His throne of mercy grew.

A breakthrough in my understanding of God came during the period when my kitchen was in a state of disrepair and had been so for several years. Wallpaper was peeling, appliances were aging. There was even a hole in the wall. What we needed was a whole new kitchen. But of course, there was no way we could afford to spend a penny on this project. At this point in my journey of knowing God, I dared not even approach God about this matter. Subconsciously, I viewed Him as distant and unconcerned about these types of problems. However, my curiosity was piqued as I noticed a verse in my Bible study that said: "You have not because you ask not. You ask and do not receive, because you ask with wrong motives" (James 4:2c–3a).

> At this point in my journey of knowing God, I dared not even approach God about this matter.

Could this verse be applied to my life circumstances? Could I ask these things of God? What if these promises were for the people of the Bible only? All these questions swirl around an ignorance of God and His ways.

Is it even okay to pray for a new kitchen? I mused to myself thinking, *Surely, God does not concern Himself with such unspiritual things.* Like most others, I thought God wasn't concerned with the "stuff" of life that concerned me. I thought my conversations with God could only be of a spiritual nature, like someone's soul. But the kitchen was in dire need of a miracle. It was such an eyesore that I began to be embarrassed about it. So I talked to God about it. Mostly those prayers were for God to help me overcome my desire for a new kitchen and be content with what I had.

My husband and I hosted many a dinner for those we were discipling, frequently having three or more single mothers for Sunday lunch. We shared Thanksgiving with those who had no family nearby. I had forgotten that Jesus spent many an evening in the dining rooms of those He came to reach. Hadn't many of His messages revolved around supper time with Zaccheus, Mary, and Martha, and more than a Pharisee or two? Jesus was certainly aware of the importance of the kitchen.

Over the years I had gotten several estimates and even took on a part-time job to cover a home improvement loan. But it seemed that God would not allow it, for He had been convicting us concerning indebtedness, teaching us to trust Him rather than run out and borrow first. For a year, I had painstakingly set aside money for my kitchen fund and began to be hopeful after saving $1,500. You can imagine how I felt when I discovered my little savings account completely emptied in one day. Though I do not remember any explanation or understanding of how it happened, I was informed that the IRS had garnished the account to pay for unpaid income taxes! Like a kick in the stomach, once again I felt hopeless about making any improvements in my life.

Meanwhile, Stan and I attended another CBMC family conference in which the speaker, Major Thomas, encouraged us to live lives of great faith, comparing it to going to the barn of God's goodness that has been stored up for those who believe God. Stan and I began to dream about how to accomplish our home improvement project. One night, fresh off the week-long conference, Stan became convinced we should move ahead with the repair of our kitchen. He tore away the peeling wallpaper with his battle cry, "We're going to the barn, Laura! We're going to the barn!"

> He tore away the peeling wallpaper with his battle cry, "We're going to the barn, Laura! We're going to the barn!"

My shredded walls remained thus for several more months as the answer always seemed to be "Wait," and "Wait some more." The project was tabled as other more pressing needs arose. Tentatively, I began to approach the subject of our kitchen to the Lord again, and my faith began to rise. Then one day while standing in the grocery store line, my eyes caught sight of a beautiful kitchen on the front of a remodeling magazine. I was so enraptured by it, I actually bought it, practically wearing out its pages, imagining that kitchen in my home. Occasionally, I showed it to my friends when they came over, as if to let them know we were aware of the state of our dilapidated diner and were eventually going to do something about it.

Then one day, I began to feel a certainty that God was going to answer my prayers very soon. I began gathering information on remodeling, and making choices. I even said to my usual diners at our Sunday lunch, "I don't know how or when, but I just know God is going to help me get a kitchen soon." The funny thing was God had already begun answering my prayer in an unusual way. A few weeks later, we found out that we were the "Grand Prize Winners" of a new kitchen!

It all began when God spoke to a young believer, Rose Wild, while she was taking a shower. She heard, "I want you to help get a new kitchen for Laura." Just like that. My sweet friend Rose, one of our little flock who had never known a stable home in her life, took on the challenge like a pro. She set up a post office box and opened a special bank account for the "Bower Kitchen Project." Then she began asking for donations in the form of a letter to our friends and family, with a very convincing verse at the top: "If anyone has material possessions and sees his brother in need but has no pity on him, how can the love of God be in him?" (1 John 3:17).

Because we had led Rose to the Lord and stood as her parents at her wedding, she and her husband, Paul, decided to make the presentation on Mother's Day. After weeks of preparation, she presented her gift to me in the form of a large card signed by the people who had contributed or volunteered in some way to remodel our kitchen. On the front of the very large poster board card were the words, "Grand Prize Winners." On the inside she pasted the magazine cover of the kitchen I adored with the salutation, "With love from Jesus and friends!" They had squeezed through our doggy door to take measurements and gather information while we were away.

At first, I was mortified and felt the humiliation of a beggar.

At first, I was mortified and felt the humiliation of a beggar. I couldn't imagine the amount of work and coordination this effort took and was amazed by the number of people who

had signed up to help. It was too much to take in. Receiving charity is a humbling experience. And yet . . . I couldn't help but squeal and laugh.

Looking at her husband in complete disbelief, I laughingly exclaimed, "Paul, why didn't you tell her we just don't do things like that!"

"If you'd seen the look on her face when she stepped out of the shower, you wouldn't be saying that. Besides, I'd rather us look like fools than disregard the voice of God," was his wise answer.

As he began to relay the rest of the story about their conversation as to the validity of hearing God's voice in a shower and how they proceeded to act in faith, I was awed by the simple obedience of this young couple. After all the years of sharing Jesus with Rose, that day the tables were turned. They became my teachers in how to trust and obey God.

What happened over the next three months was a miracle in motion. My heart was overwhelmed many times over. I witnessed God's hand move on our behalf through the lives of different people moving in and out of our kitchen, contributing in some way to this old-fashioned "barn raising." Those who could not afford money gave their time peeling wallpaper, rebuilding cabinets, painting or floating wallboard with the finale being a beautiful new kitchen that so closely resembled the magazine cover, it took me by surprise.

The Lord made a correction about one thing I was wrong about—the whole project was deeply spiritual. Once and for all, I understood there was nothing I could not come to Him about. "Now to him who is able to do immeasurably more than all we ask or imagine" (Eph. 3:20 NIV).

> He wants us to represent Him and His kingdom well. Broken down lives or houses are not what He had in mind.

I've come to trust that God is interested in all that concerns me. When you can't pay your bills or feed your kids, when you are unable to help others around you, it reflects badly on His kingdom. When you are so weighed down with the financial aspects of life you do not have the emotional energy to share your faith to advance God's kingdom, it is of concern to Him. I have come to believe that He wants us to represent Him and His kingdom well. Broken down lives or houses are not what He had in mind.

The Lesson:

Perhaps I'm not seeing amazing answers to prayers because I can't imagine what God can do for me and others I pray for. "And the LORD said, 'Behold, the people is one, and they have all one language; and this they begin to do: and now nothing will be restrained from them, which they have imagined to do'" (Gen. 11:6 KJV).

Power Principle:

The first point to know about God is that we have been given an open invitation to approach Him boldly with any of our concerns. Nothing is too big or too small to bring to Him. He is interested in the details of your life. His throne is chock full of grace and mercy for help in time of need. The problem of unanswered prayer does not lie with Him, but with us.

Prayers are hindered by a lack of confidence in our requests. We are not sure what we can or cannot ask of Him. We have not because we ask not. We do not want to appear presumptuous, so we default with the little phrase, "if it be Thy will." The question for me was this: Did my Father want me to be content with lack?

My challenge to you is this—take the time and make the effort to find out if it is His will before you charge into the work of obtaining the object of your prayer. Find His will by seeking answers in the pages of the Bible and by spending quiet time with Him. You can use the WordSpeak categories of prayer cards to jump-start your prayer life and give you confidence as you approach God's throne with His words in hand.

Next, accept the gift of imagination given to us by a generous Creator. To not use this gift would be to deny its purpose in our life. God understood that whatever people could imagine, they could accomplish when unified. That power came from a mind-set within the people. When our minds, wills, and emotions all line up, we are empowered, for good or for evil. For this reason, God gave the ancient decree to the Jews to love the Lord with all the heart, mind, and strength, not partially but totally.

To put our imaginations to use for God's purposes and plans is an outstanding use of our creative gifts.

You and God together can bring about positive changes in whatever situation you find yourself. God is about making all things new and better. Begin by asking God to help you imagine life as He would have you live it. When we enter into His mind-set we can allow ourselves to imagine a better life. Using the mind of Christ, you can allow Him to define "better" for your life. If you have never allowed yourself the permission to envision a better life in some aspect, then do so. He may cause you to imagine a life with less, freeing you from so much entanglement. He is the one who created you to imagine, dream, and hope for better.

Sure, our carnal natures can imagine some pretty outlandish and fleshly things. But to put our imaginations to use for God's purposes and plans is an outstanding use of our creative gifts. And do not forget that God is able to do immeasurably more than we could ever ask or imagine!

Chapter 22

Knowing God

If God is for us, who can be against us? He who did not spare his own Son but gave him up for us all, how will he not also with him graciously give us all things?

—Romans 8:31–32 (ESV)

A basic truth you must know about God is that He is more willing for us to succeed than any of us realizes. Our success glorifies Him, which is why He is for us, not against us.

You would do well to meditate on the truth of this passage. Mull it over. God is for you, and He will graciously give you all that you need. Do you believe this? Letting go of the lie that God is keeping something from you is difficult unless you accept this truth—God is a giver, and He is for you. These verses speak of His intentions, not mine.

You would do well to ask Him if these statements are true for you. "Are you really for me, God? Did You give Your Son for me personally? Will You also freely give me all things that I need?"

I'll never forget the day this truth sank in for me. The surrounding circumstances appeared overwhelmingly against me. Sometimes we believe the lie that if the circumstances are against us then God is against us. It is hard to come to God when we

> Sometimes we believe the lie that if the circumstances are against us then God is against us.

believe He opposes us. God only opposes the proud, and those living in sin He cannot bless (James 4:6).

I remember walking down the sidewalk when this concept interrupted my thoughts: *Wait a minute! God is for me, not against me.* I repeated the statement aloud several times as I tried to wrap my head around it. I concluded that it was true, and the circumstances that were blocking my way would have to line up with God's will and purposes for my life. Instinctively, I spoke aloud with some conviction saying, "Circumstances, get out of my way and line up with God's will and purposes for my life!"

But after years of work, it looked like I was at a dead end with no solution in sight. As I prayed and cried through the disappointment, an old chorus from Handel's Messiah came waltzing into my mind. "Lift up your heads, O ye gates, and be ye lift up, ye everlasting doors, and the King of glory shall come in." Suddenly I knew what to do. The Spirit of God had given me a course of action. I prayed aloud, "Open up gates of confusion, open up gates of darkness, and let the King of glory come in!"

As God's ambassador here on earth I am allowed to do that, to invite the King into my quandary. Darkness and confusion had to give way because Jesus said, "I am the light of the world: he that follows Me shall not walk in darkness, but shall have the light of life" (John 8:12).

Before the day was over my situation changed and the path was clear. The light that came from His presence made the difference because the King of glory is for me, not against me. The next line of Handel's famous chorus, "Who is this King of glory? The Lord strong and mighty. The Lord mighty in battle," brought with it a memory of a time that proved these verses true in my life.

My decision to run for the president of the Booster Club was not a decision lightly made. By this time my husband and I were in full-time ministry, and I was not sure I should be involved with a "secular" job that would take up so much time. I was under the mistaken idea that because it wasn't "ministry," I should not take part. Furthermore, I didn't want to get entangled in the serious problems going on in my children's school. I preferred to pray about it and leave it at that.

Even more practical was the problem of my personality. It was definitely not like me to take on a position of leadership that would require intense organizational skills and the ability to handle large sums of money. The job was mine to have as I was currently serving as vice president, the traditional route to the presidency. But would it be wise? I considered the job overwhelming and the tasks involved daunting. The election would only be a formality. But a funny thing happened on the way to the forum. The woman who acted like my friend and confidante decided to run against me and her name showed up on the ballot without even informing me. For the very first time, there would be a run-off. Everyone was shocked. There was quite a bit of bending the rules and deceit involved. Just like a real election.

I felt shaken and somewhat betrayed. Perhaps this was my way out of a responsibility that was way over my head. My son, who was involved, really wanted me to take the position. My husband, however, was dubious about my ability to do the job with everything I had going on. So I went to the Lord for wisdom and direction. I certainly did not want to fight for the position. Perhaps I should bow out gracefully to avoid dividing the group. But what did God want me to do?

> I felt shaken and somewhat betrayed. Perhaps this was my way out of a responsibility that was way over my head.

His answer came quickly within the collection of verses in my *Daily Light*. "Wait for the Lord, and He will deliver you. Be still before the Lord and wait patiently for Him; do not fret when men succeed in their ways, when they carry out their wicked schemes. You will not have to fight this battle. Take up your positions; stand firm and see the deliverance the Lord will give you."

The answer seemed clear. I would not have to fight, but should I run? The question was, did I want the job? By the time the election came around the backbiting and jockeying for position had drawn quite a crowd. Nerves drove me to reach for the *Daily Light* the morning of the election, as I was still not sure that I wasn't going to turn tail and run. The morning's reading spoke liberally of being self-controlled, putting on faith and love as a breastplate, and preparing your mind for action. I read about putting on the armor of God to extinguish the flaming arrows of the enemy. Lastly, I read about God swallowing up death, wiping away tears, and removing the disgrace of His people.

Then I knew I didn't want to go to the meeting! Though it seemed that God was encouraging me to take this on, I don't like fights. I went about my day not knowing what I would ultimately do. The evening's selection for November 8th, the night of the election, included an incredible gift of encouragement:

You, dear children, are from God and have overcome them, because the one who is in you is greater than the one who is in the world. So do not fear, for I am with you; do not be dismayed, for I am your God. I will strengthen you and help you; I will uphold you with my righteous right hand. They will fight against you but will not overcome you, for I am with you, declares the Lord.

I knew then without a doubt that I had already won the battle to come. Many showed up to vote, and somehow my opponents reinterpreted the bylaws to eliminate half of those who would most likely support me. But it did not matter. I was backed by a mightier authority and I, a most unlikely candidate, walked out of that strange election shouldering the responsibility of a president.

As I left, I was reminded of another verse included in the day's reading, "This is what the Lord says: Because the Arameans think the Lord is a god of the hills and not a god of the valleys, I will deliver this vast army into your hands." I laughed because our meeting took place in Chesterfield Valley.

You may wonder what this has to do with kingdom business. As the year progressed, I was amazed at the success of the year both financially and influentially. God had placed me there for a reason, and I prayed my way through each and every challenge. The goal of my own heart was to bring some measure of grace into a cutthroat culture. It was not an easy job, and I was astounded by the persistent backstabbing. I had never before faced such overt hostility and even name-calling.

The goal of my own heart was to bring some measure of grace into a cutthroat culture.

Through it all, I learned what it means to have God be your backer. For if God is for you, people, systems, or organizations cannot stand against you, no matter how corrupt or powerful they seem. Even in the face of major opposition, a tremendous shift in the school system happened through our influence. But that for me was not the end of the story.

A few weeks after my tenure was completed, I received a note of thanks from one of the members who I thought had no respect for me. She expressed her appreciation for a job well done by saying, "You brought such grace into the job." If nothing else had been accomplished that year, that would have been enough. "But thanks be to God, who gives us the victory through our Lord Jesus Christ" (1 Cor. 15:57).

The key to my victory was seeking God's will first and then following His lead. Patience in hearing from God and confirmation in Scripture is necessary to finding the right path. When He goes before me and reveals His will, then my prayers will follow His lead and I will simply accompany Him toward victory.

The Lesson:

When circumstances come against me, I remember that God is for me, not against me. When I follow Him, I will experience victory. "*I will go before you and make the rough places smooth; I will shatter the doors of bronze and cut through their iron bars*" (Isa. 45:2).

Power Principle:

Not understanding the character of God is a significant hindrance to our prayers because we do not understand the nature of our relationship with Him. I have experienced delight in partnering with God to bring His will into my circumstances. I have also felt at a loss in knowing how to pray. The more I know about Him and His ways, the better I am able to pray effectively.

> I have experienced delight in partnering with God to bring His will into my circumstances.

Taking the time to spend with God in prayer and Bible reading is the most productive way to know Him and His ways. Letting God speak to us through His Word is essential for staying on track in this business of living life and knowing God.

Lies about God must first be identified before you can replace them with the truth. Do you believe God is at the very least uninterested in you, or at the worst, against you? Then you are believing a lie. Kick out the lies you have harbored about God and seed your subconscious by listening to the truths of Scripture. Book 1 CD speaks the scriptures that reflect the correct images of God and yourself accompanied by music for meditation. Information on obtaining this CD can be found in the back of the book.

Commit to understanding those barriers that hinder your ability to see God as He really is. Speak the "Character of God" prayer cards to illuminate the truth and correct your subconscious beliefs. WordSpeak is not a shortcut to knowing God—that comes with spending time with Him; it is an aid to knowing His ways. If you honor God and His laws, you can safely say, "If God be for us, who can be against us?" Circumstances may appear to be against you, but God is not. Knowing that He is for us and not against us is a nugget of truth that is a treasure and brings us the confidence to wait for His answers.

Chapter 23

Our Father Who Art in Heaven

Because you are sons, God has sent forth the Spirit of His Son into our hearts, crying, "Abba! Father!"

—Galatians 4:6

Although we see in the Bible that God is a tremendous Creator and King of the universe, sometimes we forget that He is first and foremost a Father. He is the Father of creation, the Father of a nation, and Father to His only Son, Jesus. He is also our Father, but many of us have a problem with that. When our image of a loving father is skewed, it is hard to transfer our affection to God as Father. If your own father has been disapproving, harsh, unloving, absent, or worse—abusive—then you have a problem. That is why is it most important to go the Word of God with an open mind and heart and ask God to reveal Himself to you. First He must heal your wounds.

Without realizing it, that was my intent when I went to the garden at the retreat center. Or perhaps I should say, it was God's intent to reveal Himself to me the day He invited me to meet Him in the garden. I was weary after having stayed up well into the night talking with the other retreat participants. The speaker for the weekend had sensed within me a deep struggle and was very attentive to me. She prayed for me all throughout the weekend as she labored to deliver a message of a loving Father. She knew I needed to experience Him in some personal way.

"Just relax, Laura, and thank God in advance for what He is about to give you," she said cryptically.

Going back to the dormitory to try and rest, I climbed into my bunk after the other girls left our room. Everyone was excited. I desperately needed to close my eyes for a bit, but no sooner had I laid my head on the pillow than I heard this invitation in my mind:

"Come meet me in the garden."

Whew! Now I am talking to myself, I thought as I restlessly turned over to try to relax.

"Come meet me in the garden," I heard again on the other side of the pillow.

I was beginning to be irritated with myself and whispered, "I just need to get some sleep." After beginning to doze off, I sensed I was not alone. It did not feel as if I were talking to myself. One more time, I tried turning over to clear my head. But a strange awareness began to well up inside me, and I had a sobering thought. *What if that truly was the voice of God? I would hate to miss meeting Him for a nap.* So I dragged myself up, and wearily headed out to the garden.

What if that truly was the voice of God? I would hate to miss meeting Him for a nap.

The retreat center was an old convent and the "garden" wasn't well kept. In fact, I noticed that there were

no benches to sit on and no flower beds in sight. It was an overcast, balmy day. The wind was high, swirling around this so-called garden. The stately trees surrounding the area bent and swayed mightily, giving it an ominous appearance. As I approached, I noticed a strange thing. In a clearing with a clump of trees in the middle of the place, the trees were standing tall, perfectly still. A shivery feeling ran over me.

Initially I felt the sense of awe that accompanies such sights in nature, but shortly I stilled myself in the center of the garden under the peaceful trees. I began to ask myself, *How does a person encounter God?* There was no place to sit, so I walked around feeling some-what foolish for thinking that God

I began to ask myself, *How does a person encounter God?*

might possibly speak to me. Finally, I plopped down under the trees and began to pray. Then I listened. But nothing happened.

I felt abject, personally confronted with my disconnectedness from God. I wondered what I was supposed to do, but I only felt disconsolate and confused. To pass the time I naturally began to sing C Austin Miles' old hymn, *In the Garden*:

> I come to the garden alone,
> While the dew is still on the roses.
> And the voice I hear falling on my ear
> The Son of God discloses.
>
> And He walks with me and He talks with me.
> And He tells me I am His own.
> And the joy we share as we tarry there,
> None other has ever known.

Wanting desperately to hear God's voice, I stood up, suddenly realizing that I had never felt like I was one of His own. I think I must have told Him so and waited for His reply. There was only silence. So I kept on walking, trying to stir up more faith to hear God, when another song came to my mind. It was a camp song by Dennis Jernigan I had just learned from the youth of our church. The melody was lilting and the words were so different. I began to sing the strange little chorus:

> When the night is falling, and the day is done.
> I can hear you calling, "Come."
> I will come as you sing over me.
>
> "How I love you, child I love you.
> How I love you, child I love you. How I love you."

Suddenly, tears welled up. So that was it. Walking to try to make sense of my emotions, I began to talk aloud. "I know you love me, God, but honestly, I don't feel it. I feel bad for saying it but I've never felt Your love. I know I'm wrong, but I wish I could feel Your presence and Your love." More of a confession than a statement, more of a plea than a prayer, I made the statement as much to myself as to God.

I think I fully expected to hear His voice aloud. But all I heard were the words of the little chorus circling in my ears. Then it hit me, as if a lightening bolt had struck nearby. "When the night is falling, and the day is done." He was going to come to me that night in the service and do what, I did not know. I just knew I would meet Him there. The night was falling and the day was drawing to a close, and I rushed out of the garden to get prepared for the evening service. Expectancy overwhelmed me.

Sitting through the service, I wondered how and when I would encounter Him. My Bible lay on the pew beside me opened to a verse that said, "I will not leave you as orphans, I will come to you" (John 14:18). At the end of the service when an invitation for prayer was given, I felt the certain pull of the divine arms calling me to the front. Stepping out, shaking all over, I knew He would be there to meet me. He had been with me all along, of course, but using the hands and hearts of His people, He was able to touch me and hold me in His arms.

Using the hands and hearts of His people, He was able to touch me and hold me in His arms.

I could not communicate what I needed to the lovely ladies who met me up front. One prayed against fear, and a raging cry rose from my chest. The other remained with me while I sobbed silently. I could hear her praying softly beside me, and suddenly she said: "I feel as if I am hearing God speaking to you. He is saying that He wants you to meet Him in the garden, and He wants to walk with you, and that He has things He wants to share with you." Then she paused and gently said, "Oh, He says to tell you that . . . you are His very own child."

Waves of liquid love engulfed me, felling the walls around my heart. I was cocooned for several lovely moments in the middle of His love while the intercessor, who happened to be the song leader, sang over me! I cannot describe the sensation, but I truly felt overwhelmed by His love. Closing my eyes I saw a shadowy face that I took to be that of Jesus. He was so close, so personal, so loving that I didn't want to leave. The ladies surrounding me were patient and careful, leaving me alone with the Lover of my soul.

Waves of liquid love engulfed me, felling the walls around my heart.

I suppose you can say that is when I fell in love. A precious love affair began that night as God poured His love over me. That is the day I saw Jesus for who He really was, the great Lover of my soul. "Deep calls to deep in the roar of your waterfalls; all your waves and breakers have swept over me. By day the Lord directs his love, at night his song is with me" (Ps. 42:7–8).

The Lesson:

God is first of all my loving heavenly Father. He longs to be gracious to me. He calls me into a loving relationship with Him. "The LORD longs to be gracious to you, and therefore He waits on high to have compassion on you" (Isa. 30:18).

Power Principle:

Not only is God Almighty the King of the universe, He is, after all, your Father in heaven. If you do not have an accurate image of how a good father behaves with his child, the scripture cards in the "God the Father" category will help you change your perspective. You will find that like any good father, God wants to bless, guide, protect, comfort, forgive you. He is able to do all those things you cannot do for yourself.

Ask yourself this question: How do I see God? Our image of God is formed through initial family experiences. Depending on your circumstances, you may see Him as a punishing God, an absent Father, or the shaming God. You might be shocked to discover that most of us have formed God in our own image, making the object of our worship none other than an idol. The Ten Commandments expressly state that we are not to make for ourselves an idol. Though our image of God may not be carved out of stone, it might as well be.

If the God who created this universe and holds all things together is waiting for you to come to Him with your concerns, what are you waiting for?

Most of us have created the image of a false god, and it is our responsibility to replace the lies with the truth. He is not angry with you. God is not your adversary. God is bigger and more loving than any of us can imagine. If the God who created this universe and holds all things together is waiting for you to come to Him with your concerns, what are you waiting for? You must exercise the muscle of faith that believes these verses about God in the face of all conflicting reports.

Many times we have to get outside of established religion to have our views of God changed. At times the flowing robes and austere faces, implying that God's only interest in us is that we be good, misrepresent God the Father. I thank God for the many priests and ministers of the gospel who lovingly pastor their flocks, but we must be careful to separate the clergy from our image of God.

I know from experience that God is willing and able to answer your questions about Him and His ways. He is eager to enter into a lifelong conversation with you as you read His Word. My prayer is that you will begin to know the God of the Bible as He reveals Himself. Not as your family, or your opinion, or your simple ignorance has formed God in your mind, but as He really is. As you encounter God and begin to know Him, your confidence in prayer will grow.

The Truth About Yourself

If you abide in My word, then you are truly disciples of Mine; and you shall know the truth, and the truth shall set you free.

—John 8:31–32

Chapter 24

Bought and Paid For

I came that they may have life, and have it abundantly. I am the good shepherd; the good shepherd lays down His life for the sheep.

—John 10:10–11

B ut will He do it for me? This is the burning question of every heart. Most of us do not disbelieve the promises of God; we disbelieve He will do it for us personally. This is the bridge that is broken in our relationship with Christ. Will He do it for me? Can the abundant life be true for me? So much of our life and experiences have taught us otherwise, leaving ungodly belief systems unchallenged and well-entrenched. "That may be true for others, but not for me." This matter must be settled before you can receive the life God is offering you.

Late one night as I struggled to prepare for a women's retreat, I laid my head down on all my preparations, my outlines, and transparencies I had worked so hard to produce. My husband had just listened to the main points of my presentation and made a simple comment, "Sounds awfully religious. When are you going to tell them your story?"

"I don't have time for stories," I insisted. "I have to teach them the principles!" But I knew he was right. I had to start all over, so I cried out to God for help, "What am I supposed to do now?"

Straightaway I heard Him answer, "Just tell them I paid it all."

The hot tears on my face expressed what my heart understood immediately. He did not need to say more. With a contrite heart, I wept before His throne for making the message more complicated. He has paid it all, and we are not availing ourselves of the many great gifts He paid dearly for.

All that you need for your life has already been bought and paid for. You don't need to wonder if He will do it for you. He already has. He didn't just pay it all, He paid it all *for you.* You may not have felt this connection to God that I am describing. Maybe you can't hear God's voice. Consider this important passage: "You do not believe, because you are not of My sheep. My sheep hear My voice, and I know them, and they follow Me; and I give eternal life to them, and they will never perish; and no one will snatch them out of My hand" (John 10:26–28).

All that you need for your life has already been bought and paid for.

Jesus declared Himself to be "the way, the truth, and the life, and no one comes to the Father except through Me" (John 14:6). So you have a choice to make. Do you believe Him or not? "God has given us eternal life, and this life is in His Son. He who has the Son has the life; he who does not have the Son of God does not have the life" (1 John 5:11–12). When you accept Jesus, you receive this eternal life and all the blessings it brings. After you accept Jesus, you breathe in the connection to all that is good and life-giving—the Spirit of God. You become "born again" (John 3:3) and "a new creature in Christ" (1 Cor. 5:17).

After you accept Jesus, you breathe in the connection to all that is good and life-giving—the Spirit of God.

The promises offered to you as a new creature in Christ are always connected to Jesus. He came to give us life, not a miserable life, but an abundant one. With His own blood, pain, and life, He bought and paid for our release from eternal punishment and our entrance into eternal life that begins the moment we accept Jesus as our Savior.

Salvation will not automatically come to you. You must accept Jesus for yourself. Once you accept God's extravagant gift of His Son, you receive His love. His love for you explains so clearly why God was able to stand by and watch His own Son be crucified by evil men. "For God so loved the world, that He gave His only begotten Son, that whoever believes in Him should not perish, but have everlasting life" (John 3:16).

The penalty for sin and disobedience has been satisfied once and for all. Jesus' death paid for all sins, past, present, and future. God is no longer angry, and we no longer have to spend the bulk of our time atoning for our sins like the people of the Old Testament. The debt for our sin has been wiped out. What a relief!

So why did I waste so many years wading in self-condemnation? Because my mind-set needed to be changed. My heart filled with sorrow once I realized that I had not accepted nor esteemed completely what Jesus did for me on the cross. My behavior was saying to Him, "It wasn't enough. I have to beat myself up to atone." Though it felt so true, it was a devilish lie. How that must have grieved the heart of God. Once I realized that it was insulting to the redeeming work of Jesus, I revised my thinking.

> So why did I waste so many years wading in self-condemnation? Because my mind-set needed to be changed!

We do not have to be ashamed when we approach God's throne in prayer because now there is no condemnation for those who are in Christ Jesus (Rom. 8:1). If you have accepted Christ as your Savior, congratulations, you are now given the right to be called children of God (John 1:12) and nothing can separate you from His love:

> Who shall separate us from the love of Christ? Shall tribulation, or distress, or persecution, or famine, or nakedness, or peril, or sword? Neither death, nor life, nor angels, nor principalities, nor things present, nor things to come, nor powers, nor height, nor depth, nor any other created thing, shall be able to separate us from the love of God, which is in Christ Jesus.
>
> —Romans 8:35, 38–39

God is not an arbitrary despot just waiting to zap you, but a loving Father Who is intimately acquainted with your life and has plans for you. "'For I know the plans that I have for you,' declares the LORD, 'plans for welfare and not for calamity to give you a future and a hope'" (Jer. 29:11). Knowing Him as He really is, the God who cares, who offers to help with burdens, the God who provides, the God who sees your situation, who blesses and fights for you—you will run to Him with open arms.

The Lesson:

The promises of God are only true for those who believe Him and accept His Son as their Savior. When I accept Him, I receive eternal life and become connected to this abundant life that He bought and paid for. "These things I have written to you who believe in the name of the Son of God, in order that you may know that you have eternal life" (1 John 5:13).

Power Principle:

Eternal life is more than a quantity of life; it is a quality of life that Jesus bought and paid for with His life. The purpose of this book is to help you make the connection with Almighty God. The process of salvation is simple, but powerful: "If you confess with your mouth Jesus as Lord, and believe in your heart that God raised Him from the dead, you will be saved; for with the heart a person believes, resulting in righteousness, and with the mouth he confesses, resulting in salvation" (Rom. 10:8–10).

When the mind, the will and the emotions line up, the mouth will confess that Jesus is Lord, and salvation is the result. Once you understand that your sins have separated you from God and you need to be forgiven, you accept His remedy. The only process of salvation that you must do to be saved is:

Admit you are a sinner (mind).
Believe that Jesus was raised from the dead (heart).
Confess that Jesus is your Lord (mouth).

Your confession will be recorded in the heavenly book of life once you have declared it before witnesses. "Whoever confesses Me before men, him I will also confess before My Father who is in heaven. But whoever denies Me before men, him I will also deny before My Father who is in heaven" (Matt. 10:32–33).

Many people pray to God without being connected to the lifeline—Jesus Christ.

Many people pray to God without being connected to the lifeline—Jesus Christ. Prayer has been called the spiritual work of the kingdom and sometimes it is work. But it's not just business to God, it's personal. It may be hard for you to imagine that the God of the universe wants a personal relationship with you. Yet He does. In fact, He paid a high price for it.

Chapter 25

The Meditations of Your Heart

Let the words of my mouth and the meditations of my heart be acceptable in Thy sight, O Lord, my rock and my redeemer.

—Psalm 19:14

The psalmist penned an earnest plea when he prayed for help with his thoughts and words. And no wonder, for how you think influences the course of your life. What you believe about yourself determines your behavior. Over time, experience that supports your belief system forms a mind-set that becomes a fortress. Changing what you meditate on doesn't just change your mind, but also your behavior. Becoming aware of the words of your mouth and the meditations of your heart will help you harness these processes to bring good things into your life.

Nothing trumps positive outcomes to prayer quicker than a poor self-image.

When you submit your thought life to God's truth, your whole being comes into agreement with the promises of God and you will no longer be that double-minded man, unstable in all his ways. You will be able to pray for something and receive His answer because you believe it for yourself.

Beware of false perceptions of yourselves and God because they will short-circuit your prayer life. Nothing trumps positive outcomes to prayer quicker than a poor self-image.

For years I sabotaged myself and my prayer life with unconscious thoughts like these: *I'm useless. No one ever listens to me. I can't ask for that. I have to take what I can get.* The circumstances around me appeared to agree with my inward thoughts. I had to learn to love myself and choose a different way of thinking, for as he thinks in his heart, so is he (Prov. 23:7).

My in-laws' fiftieth anniversary party gave me a perfect opportunity to change the way I thought about myself. Because the initial cost to cater barbeque and beans was too high for us, I lobbied the brothers and sisters to let me coordinate the food for this great event. My mother-in-law, Jeannie Bower, had served us beautiful and bounteous dinners over the years, and I thought it only fitting that she be served a banquet fit for a queen to celebrate this milestone in her life. She had raised a family of five children, feeding them breakfast, lunch, and dinner every day while they lived in her home, baking breads and pies on a daily basis for her large bunch. No, barbeque and beans just wouldn't cut it for her.

Initially, I went to the professional caterers and picked up brochures and considered pricing. But of course, we could not afford to have such a lavish feast catered. I would have to make the dinner myself. Though each family would contribute financially, no help with the cooking and preparations would be forthcoming from the siblings for we were spread out over several states. I was the only one on the line. Interestingly enough, you would not call the culinary arts one of my strengths, nor organizing and time manage-ment my strong suits. On the contrary, my ability to get discombobulated was renowned. But out of love and respect for my in-laws, I took on the job.

I set about learning the ins and outs of catering a large party, acquiring the skills along the way. There was no time to practice. I developed a strategy that proved to be brilliant. I constantly prayed a desperate prayer, seeking to prove its message to myself and those who were trusting me to pull this off. "I can do all things through Christ who strengthens me" (Phil. 4:13 NKJV).

With the help of the caterer's brochures and the pans and advice from the ladies in the church kitchen, I set about planning how much food to buy and when. The event would be out of town, and the details of the party a surprise, no less. I would have to find a way to transport the huge amount of food, store it for a day, and find a spacious kitchen to work in away from my in-laws' home. How I could coordinate the peeling of the shrimp, the roasting of the beef, the carving of the garnishes, and the display of the spread was beyond my imagination.

But I did have the brochures to look at, and I studied them over and over to get the picture in my head of what this should look like. Each time I made the decision to buy the food, pick the pans, coordinate the timing, I breathed this prayer, "Lord, You said I can do all things through Christ who gives me strength. Help me make the right decisions."

The day before we were to leave, I began to experience subtle panic attacks, and I received some of the best advice from the one of the precious cooks in our church kitchen. "Honey, it's too late to be worrying now. Don't think, just do. Don't think, just do."

"What if I don't know what to do?" I replied.

> "Honey, it's too late to be worrying now. Don't think, just do."

"Just do the next thing, next," was her sage advice.

So taking her advice, I went on auto pilot, breathing my scripture just like the "little engine that could."

"I can do all things through Christ, I can do all things through Christ."

The party was a hit! Not simply because of the lavish and tasty spread (no catastrophes, I might add), but because there was such joy in the final preparations. I took charge of the church's kitchen like a pro, delegating this job to one brother and that job to the sisters. We laughed and went about putting together a feast for a king like it was child's play. In the end, there were no worries, no last-minute crises, and all went well.

After we laid out the beautiful prime rib roast, perfectly pink in the middle, the shrimp cocktail over crushed ice in a shining silver punch bowl, coordinated with a variety of vegetables in all colors, and shaped garnishes carved to look like umbrellas, my mother-in-law gasped and covered her mouth in the characteristic way she did when trying not to burst into tears. Never had we pulled off such a wonder before. We could all see that she got the message we wanted to convey—she was loved and greatly appreciated.

> My mother-in-law gasped and covered her mouth in the characteristic way she did when trying not to burst into tears.

I went home exhausted but satisfied. One more time I was completely bonded with the Lord. As for my self-image, it would take a few more successes like this one to convince me to change the way I thought about myself. I was much more comfortable feeling incompetent than capable. A major work had to be done from within. I had to commit to that work with God's help and the help of Christian counselors.

At first, I was unaware of the negative remarks going on in my head. I certainly wasn't living life conscious of my thoughts. Even though God's Word directed me to think otherwise, it "took some doing," as my kinfolk used to say. The old way of thinking was so entrenched I did not recognize the negative patterns for a long time. They had become a part of who I was.

The Bible really did mess with my impoverished thought processes and I am ever so grateful. As I read the Bible with this new mind-set, I noticed that much of the conversation between God and His chosen people reads like a love letter. When I personalized the verses, it changed me. As I caught the message of God's love for me, a particular verse touched my heart: "I am my beloved's and my beloved is mine" (Song of Sol. 6:3).

The Bible really did mess with my impoverished thought processes and I am ever so grateful.

The Lesson:

When I dwell on God's Word I get His perspective. When I bind my mind, my will, and my emotions to the mind of Christ, my thoughts about myself will line up with the truth. "Be transformed by the renewing of your mind." (Rom. 12:2b).

Power Principle:

As Christians we must take responsibility for our thought life and our words. Most do not acknowledge the power of thought that God placed in each of us as He created us in His own image. Just like our concept of God, our own image is formed through early family experiences, good and bad. Wrong self-image is as much a hindrance to our prayers as misunderstanding the character of God. If you struggle with low self-worth, it will be hard for you to accept all the great and magnificent promises God has offered to you. You may even sabotage the positive answers that are brought your way.

In my school days we had an event called "Turnabout," where the girls had a chance to ask out the boy for a change. Getting to choose was wonderfully refreshing. The same can be true with our thoughts. Instead of passively allowing wrong thoughts to run the gamut, we can become aware of negative self-talk and exchange it for right thoughts. By meditating on the WordSpeak

Self-Image prayer cards and speaking them aloud, you can make new grooves in your mind, giving you an alternate way of thinking.

When you catch an unproductive thought and replace it with the Word of God, you are destroying speculations and every lofty thing raised up against the knowledge of God, and you are taking every thought captive to the obedience of Christ (2 Cor. 10:5). You may need to start at the beginning with the thought that God made you in His image—male and female (Gen. 1:26). Even more personally God said, "Before I formed you in the womb, I knew you" (Jer. 1:5). Speaking these truths aloud will startle you into thinking differently about yourself and your relationship with God: *I am made like God. He knew me before I was born. I am His workmanship.* The self-image category of WordSpeak offers several verses that underscore your worth and value to God.

Taking Scripture personally and expecting God to speak to you through the Bible will change you. Clearing away the debris from poor self-image will not only give you peace and confidence but also help you hear God more clearly. You must not allow feelings of inferiority to remain. They go against who you really are in Christ. I now believe that possessing poor self-image and wrong images of God are the greatest hindrances to living the abundant life. If we really understood how God sees us, we would pray with much more boldness and authenticity.

Chapter 26

The Words of Our Mouths

*By your words you will be justified and by your words you will be
condemned.*

—Matthew 12:38

Wile you tackle the remodeling of your mind-set, you must also
monitor what is coming out of your mouth. Words are not just
simply vehicles that expose beliefs. Our words have a God-ordained power
behind them. What we confess is a critical part of setting prayers into motion.

What if we said it this way—by your
words your prayers will be justified,
and by your words your prayers will
be condemned? That might make us
think twice about what comes out of
our mouths. Even mindless negative
statements clutter the consciousness
and bring static to the airwaves.
Instead of our words working against
our prayers, we should harness this
power for good. Praying one way and saying another is like "talking out of
both sides of your mouth."

Our words have a
God-ordained power
behind them.

Words actually help us form opinions of ourselves. Repeated over time,
words become sculptors of our self-image. What have you been saying about
yourself all these years? Or what have those in authority over you as a child
said about you? Is there a consistency between those words and your reality?

You may need to "renounce" any negative statements and "re-announce" that now only that which God's Word says about you is true and will come to pass. Sometimes the battle against well-established negative patterns in our lives is fought by changing what comes out of our mouths. "But the things that come out of the mouth come from the heart, and these defile you" (Matt. 15:18).

After reading some illustrations of this concept of negative words becoming reality, I began to ask God about a certain indictment spoken over my husband by a parent. "He'll never be able to earn enough because he is not a professional." Stan and I had jokingly repeated these words in both productive and unproductive seasons of our life together. When I became aware of the power of negative words, I asked the Lord to reveal the nature of this pronouncement. Could mere words have a negative impact on our life? After all, we did seem to be in a constant struggle to rise above the bar of insufficiency. I asked God to give me an answer in a dream. "You gave people in the Bible dreams, why not me?" was the logic I used.

Could mere words have a negative impact on our life?

Soon after, my husband began to tell me of a "very vivid dream" he had that night. Our family was trapped in our station wagon as dangerous floodwaters of the bayou threatened to engulf us. His dilemma was whether to roll the windows down before or after the car went under, in an effort to save us. As he pondered his dilemma, he saw some water-skiers all dressed in black being pulled behind a boat doing stunts over a ramp. After watching them a while, he said to himself, "I can do that." But then he stopped himself, saying, "No, those guys are professionals. I'm not a professional."

I about dropped the scrambled eggs I was preparing for breakfast.

"Bizarre, isn't it?" my husbanded concluded calmly as he finished tying his necktie and walked out of the room. He had no idea of the impact of his words. As the dream unfolded, he repeated those deadly words that I had put before the Lord. I had not shared my request with a living soul, certainly not him.

As soon as everyone left for school and work, I immediately went to God for confirmation. "Is this legitimate?" I asked. You may find this laughable, but at this point I was new at hearing from God. Technically, I had asked God to give *me* the dream, and I wanted to be sure I was interpreting this correctly.

Surely as I am writing this, in my thoughts I heard this answer, *It would be natural for you to dream it. You would have dismissed it as a subconscious thought.*

By giving the dream to my husband, it became a supernatural revelation. If I had dreamt it, I would have dismissed it. Of course I dreamt it, it was in the back of my mind. But it wasn't in the back of Stan's mind. Though I probably couldn't convince anyone else, I was certain of the toxic nature of these words, and God began to show me how to reverse them. From this point on, my husband and I renounced any negative pronouncements we became aware of and replaced them with positive words from Scripture.

Whatever negative truths said about you can be left behind. You no longer have to agree with negative pronouncements, however true they seem. You can come out of agreement with them by saying, "Perhaps that was true of me in the past, but now I am (fill in the blank)." No matter what we pray, our mouths generally announce what will be. No wonder that the Spirit of God inspired King David to pen this prayer. "Set a guard, O Lord over my mouth; keep watch over the door of my lips" (Ps. 141:3).

You no longer have to agree with negative pronouncements, however true they seem.

The Lesson:

I can harness the power of my words to speak God's will and purposes into existence. I can become what God says I am. "Death and life are in the power of the tongue" (Prov. 18:21).

Power Principle:

When we take God's Word, believe it in our hearts, and declare it aloud, we are actually aligning ourselves with God's purposes by using a very powerful spiritual law. Woven into the fabric of God's creation are many physical and spiritual laws, which though unseen, work with indisputable accuracy. The law of gravity, an invisible yet compelling force, may be hard to explain. Yet even a child learns to respect this law of nature when he tries to "fly" and falls to the ground. As he grows in understanding of this law of nature, he can begin to harness its power and use it for good or for evil.

Likewise, many spiritual laws are at work even if we are ignorant of them. One such law gives power to our words. We can use our words to bless or we can use our words to curse (James 3:10). Social science has long since acknowledged the power of negative words over young children. If a parent repeatedly calls a child "dumb" or "thickheaded" the child will be bent in that direction. The reverse is also true. Positive words bless the hearer and encourage him or her to act accordingly. The genius of the WordSpeak prayer card system is that it gives us the positive words we need to cooperate with the Word of God to bring the will of God into our particular circumstances. It may take some time, but it will come to pass.

Positive words bless the hearer and encourage him or her to act accordingly.

Sometimes we cannot help but speak negative words when we see negative realities around us. When we see a bad situation, I believe we must speak honestly and call it what it is. But we must be careful not to draw wrong conclusions. For instance, each time my husband and I locked horns, I concluded in exasperation, "We are hopeless!" because it seemed so very true. But I was actually speaking a lie. God convicted me about this statement when I read this verse: "What is impossible with man is possible with God" (Luke 18:27).

I remember when it first occurred to me that my personal quagmire was not beyond the reach of God. I had often referred to the verse in Jeremiah 32:17b, "Nothing is too difficult for Thee," without associating this powerful statement with relationship problems. I discovered that often my mind-set and my resolute words kept my problems away from the Source of help. I had to change my mind and watch my words. Difficult relationships are not impossible for God to fix. As I endeavored to counsel with men and women over the years I offer this scripture to bolster their flagging confidence, "Nothing is too difficult for God, not even us!"

The Truth About Power

For the kingdom of God does not consist in words but in power.

—1 Corinthians 4:20

Chapter 27

Power of the Spoken Word

For assuredly, I say to you, whoever says to this mountain, "Be removed and be cast into the sea," and does not doubt in his heart, but believes that those things he says will be done, he will have whatever he says.

—Mark 11:23

Although I was familiar with this scripture, I never really understood its meaning for my life. I doubt most Christians do. But one day I noticed how many times Jesus repeated the word *says* in this statement. He will have whatever he says is an extraordinary offer no matter what the conditions. I experienced the truth taught here by Jesus long before I understood the principle. My transformation from being a person without much of a voice to becoming a woman of influence was based on the principle of this verse.

I heard the Lord speak quietly to me, "Look at their faces." Slowly, I raised my eyes to meet their gaze.

The day I stood on the stage of an open-air auditorium in Costa Rica was a turning point for me. I was only a handyman, called up to hold the tapes of the messages given to those who came forward for prayer. Struggling with self-consciousness, I kept my head down, focused on my job. Trying to get my usual shaking under control, I heard the Lord speak quietly to me, "Look at their faces." Slowly, I raised my eyes to meet their gaze.

Looking into the defeated faces of the nearly three hundred women changed me. Their slumped shoulders and weary eyes told me they could not take in the message being preached that day. These were the abused women of Costa Rica we had traveled so far to help. Some had been forced into prostitution, their little children playing around their feet. I was struck by their hopelessness and helplessness. No amount of inspired words coming from our teacher that day could help them in their private hells.

"You have something to give them. You have a weapon to put in their hands," I heard Him say. Feeling as if God's arm was around my shoulders as we observed these women, courage rose in my soul. And then I knew.

Indeed, I did have a weapon that I could share with women who needed a special kind of help. I stood tall with the dignity that God gives. I had something to give to these women to help them fight their personal battles in which they felt so alone.

Feeling as if God's arm was around my shoulders as we observed these women, courage rose in my soul.

A determination was born that day to complete this work, WordSpeak, with its message and prayer cards, and take it back to that country. It was very

personal to me because I had experienced so much victory in my own home by taking God's Word, believing it and speaking it over my circumstances. My home is very different now from the way it used to be. The beginning of our life together was fraught with intense anger and division, with plenty of strife in the atmosphere among everyone.

From sibling rivalry to frequent arguments between Stan and me, it was not a place of peace. It sickened me, but I could not stop the violent outbursts that invaded my home space. Destruction of esteem lurked in every corner of our house. Having been raised in an angry environment, my husband had been molded by habits of anger and carried deep wounds that had not yet been healed. He described himself as "intense," but he was really just angry with the world. When we dated I had lovingly called him "my angry young man," thinking I could soothe his hurts.

But of course, I could not. He was angry inside, and it spilled out onto us. I became angry at him. It was no wonder that the kids followed suit. You can be sure I cried out to God for help with my home, feeling powerless to stop the cycle of hurt. God intervened by teaching me the principle of declaration that I learned at a women's conference. One of the speakers told us that before we could deal with sibling rivalry we must first deal with the spiritual atmosphere of our homes. I was all ears. She shared a verse that she prayed aloud over her home, which said: "Violence will not be heard again in your land, nor devastation or destruction within your borders; but you will call your walls salvation, and your gates praise" (Isa. 60:18).

Immediately, I began to pray that this verse would be true in my house. My silent prayer went something like this, *God, please don't let violence dwell in my land, but make my walls be called "salvation" and my gates "praise,"* as if it were God's responsibility. The prayer felt vaguely inaccurate.

One particularly stressful morning when everyone seemed to be at each other's throats, I couldn't wait until everyone left the house. As soon as the door closed behind them I began to declare this verse in my own words, vehemently. Having kept my emotions under control for long enough, it was now my turn to be angry.

"Violence!" I shouted as I slammed cabinet doors, "you will no longer dwell in my land. Neither will destruction or wasting away! My walls will be called salvation and my gates praise!"

> "Violence!" I shouted as I slammed cabinet doors, "you will no longer dwell in my land."

Instinctively, I waved my hand in the air as if to paint my walls with "salvation" and over the doors and windows as if to christen them "praise." Nobody taught me to act in this manner. I didn't think about it. My body simply began to behave in accordance with the intention of that verse. I had had enough! If violence were a spirit dwelling in my land, it had to go and take with it its pals, destruction and ruin.

Suddenly, it felt as if my powerlessness had been replaced with authority. I sensed the certain reality of gained ground by declaring God's Word to be true in my land. Things changed, first in me, then in others around me. The atmosphere in my home changed, not all at once, but noticeably. Violent arguments were no longer heard in my land on any regular basis. I had entered into a new phase of my prayer life. If two began to argue, I simply prayed this prayer out loud, usually quietly or in the other room and immediately angry conversations dissipated. I can without a doubt look back to that time as a turning point in our home. All was not perfect, but it seemed that real progress with angry attitudes began at that point in our lives.

I continue to "paint" my walls salvation and my gates praise and pray that my home will be a sanctuary of peace for all who enter. If you peeked in my home on any given day, you would most likely find peace and laughter. No one would guess how far we had come. As the many guests come and go, I hear on a regular basis what a pleasure it is to be in our home. Just recently, one of my daughter's friends noted, "There's something different about your house. It's like I feel safe there."

"There's something different about your house. It's like I feel safe there."

God placed in my mouth the powerful weapon of His Word and I would never again hesitate to use it. Interestingly enough, the happiest soul in our home these days is my husband. He fills our home with flowers and cards of encouragement. We laugh and say that he has become annoyingly chipper! Now that's a good problem to have. "Therefore, take up the full armor of God, that you may be able to resist in the evil day, and having done everything, to stand firm. And take . . . the sword of the Spirit, which is the word of God" (Eph. 6:13,17).

The Lesson:

When I take God's Word to heart and declare it over my circumstances, the atmosphere will change, and God's kingdom will come. "Now to Him who is able to do exceeding abundantly beyond all that we ask or think, according to the power that works within us" (Eph. 3:20).

Power Principle:

After this experience, I came to appreciate the "power that works within us." What is that power? It begins with a mind-set formed in us by what we meditate on. When we meditate on God's Word and come to believe what God says about us, we take on a new attitude of authority. Authority comes when you accept that you have been made in God's image and that you have been made complete in Christ (Col. 2:9–10). Barriers fall and attitudes change when you stand against them with all that is within you, armed with the Word of God.

There is, of course, a reason why our voices are so powerful. It is found in the God-ordained purpose for each of our lives, a purpose that is as historic as

Adam and Eve's. The same mandate God gave to them, He gives to us: Here is your life, now make something of it. Here is your time and space, now bring it into order.

Perhaps you are not a fighter by nature. Or you might fight too much in the wrong way. You can learn to fight the battles of your life effectively by going to God first with your problem, asking Him for wisdom, seeking His answers in His Word, and then declaring God's Word to be true. Battle your problems using the sword of the Spirit, which is the Word of God, and you will see them crumble.

> The same mandate God gave to them, He gives to us: Here is your life, now make something of it.

God's Spirit will blow through you when you speak His Word and supply your own emotional energy. When you care deeply about a situation, your emotions can be used for good or evil. You must become battle-ready with the discipline of reading God's Word, obeying Him, and surrendering to His will. Once you understand His will and ways, you will become an effective prayer warrior. When you get your marching orders, you can become the voice of truth that challenges difficult circumstances. You may be the only voice of truth in the midst of chaos.

I have found that most battles are won or lost in private. The more effective I am in my prayer closet, the quicker barriers fall. Barriers fall when I confront them before the throne of God, where the effective, fervent prayer of a righteous man truly accomplishes much. The day I made the discovery of this principle, I hit my head with my hand. Of course! Why hadn't I seen it before? What we believe affects how we pray, and what we say affects the answers we receive. We are participants in answers to prayer. When our beliefs, our prayers, and our words line up, mountains can be moved! When we take the Word of God and speak it over our circumstances, problems get solved and barriers fall. Now that is the power of voice!

> When our beliefs, our prayers, and our words line up, mountains can be moved!

Chapter 28

Power of Permission

Ask and it will be given to you; seek and you will find; knock and the door will be opened to you. If you then, being evil, know how to give good gifts to your children, how much more will your Father who is in heaven give what is good to those who ask Him!

—Matthew 7:7, 11

You and I have come full circle. By now, you understand these powerful words of permission given to each member of God's family. Do you need something? Do you desire something? Then proceed through the ASK process. You do not have to feel sheepish anymore if you belong to Christ. "If you belong to Christ, then . . . you are heirs according to promise" (Gal. 3:29). You have the full rights of an heir to ask for his inheritance. The "Permission Package" of WordSpeak cards will give you all you need to navigate the prayer process. Listen to book one CD to hear the ASK promises and lodge them into your subconscious. I have been living out this abundant life for years now and am committed to share the good news with my fellow family members.

When my husband and I moved to St. Louis to take the position of full-time staff for CBMC, we struggled to find a house we could afford. Having taken years to get out of debt, we were very careful about our expenses. After several months of looking, we realized the impossible situation we were facing. Not only did we have to pay the costs of the move, we would also have to purchase jackets, blankets, and snowshoes in the transition from the tropics to the north.

So when my ten-year-old daughter asked me if she could have her own room when we moved to St. Louis, I hesitated. She roomed with her baby sister, who frequently woke her up at night, and it seemed logical that she should get a room of her own. She was, in fact, nine years older than her baby sister. But her two older brothers had seniority, both being adolescents, and they had shared a tiny room all their lives.

"But can't we even pray about it?" she asked innocently. Of course we could. But honestly, I was afraid to ask God, for this would mean we would need a house with five bedrooms. To complicate matters, we would often be hosting other CBMCers from around the country, and we would need somewhere to put our guests. The last year of our life in Houston, Stan earned a generous income and we were finally able to throw off the last vestiges of our indebtedness. While our beginning salary for the new ministry position would be a little more than one-fourth the amount Stan was currently making, the housing market in St. Louis was easily double that of our current city. We were already having a hard time finding anything remotely large enough that we could afford. We were committed to staying within our budget, but the situation seemed impossible.

I had to let go of my logical, adult thinking and do exactly what the Lord had given us permission to do—ask. So Jennie and I began praying for our new house. I wanted an expanse of land, a place for guests, and a desk for me. She wanted her own bedroom. Nightly, we prayed the same prayer. I let go of the habit of praying only for what I thought possible and delved into the realm of the impossible.

> I let go of the habit of praying only for what I thought possible and delved into the realm of the impossible.

Finally, after eighteen months of praying and looking, our house in Houston sold. Within a month we had to move. We had found a modest house in St. Louis on a fourth of an acre that had four bedrooms upstairs and a fifth bedroom in the basement. The basement had been beautifully finished with built-in cabinets and a desk. A bathroom and living area made it perfect for guests. This had to be the answer to our prayers, but we could not afford the asking price, and the sellers were not budging. After some negotiation, Stan and I decided to start over.

No other homes in our price range became available, and we seemed to be at a dead end. A fellow CBMCer in the suburbs who couldn't sell his family's home after three years, agreed to let us stay in their home rent-free for a year until we could find a house. Their house was huge, easily triple the amount we could pay. My husband talked with the owners and negotiated some terms, but his concern was for their family. He knew they desperately needed to sell their house and committed to pray for them.

Returning to St. Louis to look for a home, an interesting thing happened while I was on the trail. After asking the Lord for guidance I heard the answer in my head, *You pick the house, and I'll pay for it.* As God is my witness, these were the words I heard. However, my husband wasn't willing to plunk down money on a house based on my assertion.

"But He gave me permission," I insisted. I wanted the house with five bedrooms, but I wouldn't insist on it for I had lived too long under the burden of indebtedness to ever want to be in that mess again. So I continued to pray that God would find a place for us.

One day while washing dishes at my sink, I looked out the window and realized that each time I did, I was seeing in my mind's eye the backyard of the house in St. Louis. I wasn't seeing our backyard, I was seeing the tree in backyard of the house we could not afford. Then it dawned on me—that was our house! I believed it with all my heart, so I began thanking God for my new home. I had no doubt about it.

We began the process of packing up our house, and Stan decided to make another offer on the five-bedroom house. We agreed that it would be ours only if the owners accepted our counter offer, which they did not. Now we were in a quandary. Would we be out of line by going forward? I sat quietly, confident in the permission God had given me.

We closed our life in Houston, and began the three-week journey to our new home, heading for the rent-free house in St. Louis. During this transition period, God began moving in a different way. Friends and family began to contribute money to our future house. Each one in different ways gave money to send us off. Some gave with no knowledge of our predicament. In the end, an incredible event happened. The house offered to us rent-free, sold right out from under us. We were literally moving to St. Louis, not knowing where we were going to live.

We were literally moving to St. Louis, not knowing where we were going to live.

Stan had advised the owner of the rent-free house to "walk his land" like the Joshua walk of the Bible, consecrating it to the Lord. So many tragedies had occurred in that home that it seemed to have a black cloud hanging over it. The husband walked the land, dedicated it to the Lord, and the home sold within a few days. He was so thrilled, he offered us $12,000 for the rent or purchase of a new home. The Lord was accomplishing His word to me.

Along with the sale of our home, we received over $40,000 to put toward the purchase of our five-bedroom home, with the tree in the backyard, on a fourth of an acre. The Lord had given me incredible permission. I picked the house, and all these years He has continued to pay for it. "And this is the confidence which we have before Him, that if we ask anything according to His will, He hears us. And if we know that He hears us in whatever we ask we know that we have the requests which we have asked from Him" (1 John 5:15).

When my daughter and I prayed with childlike faith, God heard us. He gave us the desires of our hearts because He loves us. When Jennie asked me to pray for our house, I almost didn't for fear of disappointing her. I forgot that God said He would freely give us all things (Rom. 8:32). I don't understand how He can say that to His children and not risk great disappointment, but I also trust Him to give us only what is best for us.

The Lesson:

I have God's permission to ask Him for anything in the name of Jesus. "For the Lord is a sun and a shield; the Lord gives grace and glory; no good thing does He withhold from those who walk uprightly" (Ps. 84:11).

Power Principle:

God is our supreme Authority and yet, as our Father, He has given us the highest form of permission—the right to ask Him for anything in the name of Jesus (John 14:13). Permission is not just granted but is extended in the form of an invitation, by virtue of your relationship to Him as His child.

As His child, you are so important to God. You have been given a time and place in this world to accomplish your purpose. No one else can fulfill your purpose for you. Knowing this and that God hears you as you pray will immediately improve your self-worth. Who are you? I don't know you, but God does. He knows what you are capable of and what He created you to be. He offers you a place in His family, a place in His kingdom, and an opportunity to do the job you were created to do. He gives you the authority and the power to do it.

Therefore, we simply ask for God to reveal His heart on any matter we are praying about. Our hearts' desires are very much a part of this process of praying, too. Don't leave out your heart's desire, because it is the essence of who you are. Don't be afraid to talk to Him about what you want, because He has your best interest at heart. That means that if we do not get what we have asked for, we can trust that it would not have been good for us. The Lord is a sun and a shield for us.

He offers you a place in His family, a place in His kingdom, and an opportunity to do the job you were created to do.

However, when our prayer finally lines up with His will and purposes, and when our heart's desires resonate with His heart's desire, then boom! The request is granted. The problem of our prayer life is that we are so busy praying with our heads down that we don't get our minds into God's sphere. The WordSpeak Prayer Cards can help you with God's perspective.

In order to do your job of interceding for yourself, your loved ones, your business associates, your community—in effect, your world—you must have permission to communicate with God about anything and everything you need. At times you will need wisdom. At other times you will need strength. Sometimes you will need assistance, and sometimes you will need the resources to accomplish your job, whatever that is at the moment. Some periods of your life will require healing of mind, body, and/or spirit. You have been given permission to ask for all that you need. And by the way, He doesn't just care about your mission and purpose in life, He also cares about you. "Delight yourself in the Lord; and He will give you the desires of your heart" (Ps. 37:4).

The problem of our prayer life is that we are so busy praying with our heads down that we don't get our minds into God's sphere.

Chapter 29

Power of Transformation

Therefore, if any man is in Christ, he is a new creature; the old things passed away; behold, new things have come.

—2 Corinthians 5:17

You do not have to worry about whether you are the right person for the job of praying for God's kingdom to come and His will to be done. You do not have to concern yourself with the outcome of your prayers. When you yielded your heart to Jesus, you were given divine DNA. You have been empowered to communicate freely with God Almighty. Your voice has been commissioned for His service. Your desires will begin to line up with the new creation you are in Christ. Even the darkness you may have to endure has been purposed for your transformation. I can attest to that as well.

> Your voice has been commissioned for His service.

As I sat on the cool wooden bench in the woods near my counselor's office feeling unhinged, the question rose up, "Am I losing my mind?" Thinking I was late for my counseling session, I had abruptly cut off a luncheon date and rushed to my appointment, only to find I had arrived an hour early. So I sat down to collect myself. The emotional confusion of the last few days had taken a toll, and I let the tears flow.

Suddenly, a pair of small powder blue butterflies startled me, distracting me from my despair. Inadvertently, I laughed at their playful dance, reminding me not to take my recent mistake too seriously. Somehow I knew they were tiny messengers of God sent to interrupt my day. Enthralled by their flights of fancy, I sensed that God had something to say to me. Their presence made me feel less alone in my sadness and somehow brought me hope.

Suddenly, a pair of small powder blue butterflies startled me, distracting me from my despair.

The encounter with these lovely little creatures stayed with me throughout the day. I wondered how they came to be so pretty. After a little research I discovered that these little flowers-in-motion begin life as ugly, hairy caterpillars with nothing more

to live for than to eat compulsively. Then one day when their appetite is sated, they back themselves into a corner, so to speak, by encasing themselves with threads that form a cocoon. Or so I thought.

I discovered that a butterfly does not come from such a mundane dwelling as a cocoon, which breeds only a moth—but is born out of a chrysalis where a supernatural process occurs. Every moment in the chrysalis is significant. From the moment the caterpillar is confined in the chrysalis, its body begins to die. Not just wither, but it actually melts away, digested, if you will, from the inside out. Once the process begins, the caterpillar remains perfectly still until its body becomes a "soup." But there is momentum in the stillness and transformation in the chemistry. Within this liquid lies the DNA of a remarkable creature. Microscopic cells called "imaginal buds" accomplish an amazing feat—the creation of a butterfly.

Once the process begins, the caterpillar remains perfectly still until its body becomes a "soup."

Although I understood God was speaking to me, I wasn't sure how to interpret the information. It wasn't until a few weeks later I would understand. I encountered the Word

of God in such an unexpected way that I knew without a doubt the meaning of my beautiful lesson. My husband had asked me to accompany him on a trip to touch base with some of our faithful supporters. He wanted me to share a report on my perspective of the ministry, but I politely declined. In the audience would be friends and family that did not need to know how discouraged I really was. To be perfectly clear, I felt like a failure. We had been in ministry for ten years. Slowly, I had become withdrawn from ministry and social activities, feeling an emotional fatigue I could not put a finger on. God had gently led me into this purposeful wilderness in order to settle some old scores. I had heard Him say to me, "Behold, I will allure her, bring her into the wilderness, and speak kindly to her" (Hosea 2:14).

I had long since settled the issue of God's care and provision for our family and had come to understand how God could turn an imperfect couple such as us into a useful tool. But God was asking me to trust Him in this deeper work that I did not understand. The constant assault of migraines that began in earnest ten years before, and assorted physical afflictions drained me of the vigor I needed to be able to give to others. I found myself in a very dark place, wondering why I could not manifest the healing Jesus had bought for me.

"What is wrong with me?" became my mantra.

"What is wrong with me?" became my mantra. Although I felt God's presence in my solitary confinement, the inevitable demands of life became overwhelming. I had nothing good to share with this group of supporters. Or so I thought. The morning of the event as I was reading my Bible, I was arrested by these words of Jesus: "I have come as light into the world, that everyone who believes in Me may not remain in darkness" (John 12:46).

A "wow" rose up in my consciousness, a quickening in my spirit. Although I was in a dark depression, I didn't need to fear. Suddenly I realized this was a part of life and I did not have to apologize for being here. Nor did I have to stay there either, for he "who believes in Me may not remain in darkness." The revelation of it spilled out as if before my eyes. There would be an end to my darkness. Jesus would light my way. Now this was a promise I could hold onto; this was a hope I could share. More than ever I realized there was purpose in this dark place. I was in my very own chrysalis!

More than ever I realized there was purpose in this dark place. I was in my very own chrysalis!

Instantly, the lesson became crystal clear. The chrysalis is actually a tomb, a place of living death where a caterpillar that formerly could only crawl around preoccupied with eating is transformed into a beautiful creature that will fly away to a world the caterpillar could never have imagined. Somehow I understood that God would use this time of sadness and stillness to cause my false self to disintegrate! My heart flipped a bit as I imagined the freedom of flying to worlds unknown to me. Once the process was complete, I would have wings.

I thank God for a trustworthy counselor, who walked with me through old memories and helped me process the pain of life. God provided a guide to navigate these dangerous waters. If we do not face the inevitable wounds of life and unmet needs, we are left with unprocessed fears and belief systems that raise themselves up against the knowledge of God. I believe that these become the rocky places of our soil that prevent the Word of God from taking root and bearing fruit (Luke 8:6).

This personal work of God has taken time and as of this writing, I continue to walk with Him through it. But now I can see a light at the end of the tunnel. I will emerge to testify of the validity of God's Word. I trust that the process is like the metamorphosis of a once base creature into one that can fly. I pray that every moment of pain counts; that the hurt signals some change in me. I believe there are "imaginal" cells within me waiting for the falseness to give way to an unimaginable transformation. I believe that in this

I pray that every moment of pain counts; that the hurt signals some change in me.

dark place the presence of God will heal me. I trust Him to make me a new creature in Christ. I trust that for you as well.

To my surprise, I felt myself rise to share a few words at the appreciation luncheon for our guests, and the typical trembling began to overwhelm me. *Oh, no you don't,* I said to myself, *"we're not doing this!"* Instantly the trembling stopped. With an uncommon poise, I spoke a simple message of promise and hope that when we find ourselves in the shadowy places, Jesus promised to light our way. My little friends, the butterflies, were central to the message, and after I sat down I noticed that many tears of understanding had sprung up in the eyes of the audience. They had their own dark places.

I felt victory that day because I came out of my hiding place and spoke the Word of God anyway, while the clouds still hung over my head. Encouragement was delivered through a simple scripture and a brief encounter with some butterflies. All of us at the luncheon experienced His abiding love and presence in a powerful way. I saw God move with precision. His Word, living and active and sharper than any two-edged sword, cut through all the pretense and pierced our hearts. I walked away different somehow, confident that I would not just be okay, but useful to the King of kings. "Behold, I am making all things new" (Rev. 21:5).

The Lesson:

Speak God's Word over yourself or your situation while you are still in the dark, and watch the transformation take place. Keep on speaking until the light dawns. "You did not choose Me but I chose you, and appointed you that you would go and bear fruit, and that your fruit would remain, so that whatever you ask of the Father in My name He may give to you" (John 15:6).

Power Principle:

I have chosen to obey the message of this verse and now it is your turn to choose. Where will you go to bear the fruit that remains for all eternity? I know that wherever that is, you must learn to go first to your prayer closet and ask the Father whatever you wish. He has chosen you to ASK for certain favors. He has chosen you to ASK for a specific group of people in a specific time and place.

But first you must do this for yourself because the Bible says, "Freely you have received, freely give" (Matt. 10:8). Take charge of your well-being by taking a promise that you need and declaring it over your life. We cannot wait until Sunday to hear the Word of God because we need to hear it every day of our lives. We must become the priests and prophets of our own lives. We must tend to our own gardens. We must sow the seeds!

> Take charge of your well-being by taking a promise that you need and declaring it over your life.

Simply reading this book won't bring transformation, but it is a start. You can be transformed by the renewing of your mind and by the encounters with God through His Word and His world. We must listen to the voice of truth that tells a different story. When the Word of God speaks, it must first speak to us. We hear it, believe it, and come into agreement with it. Then we decide what we are going to do with that Word. Hide it in our hearts? Definitely, for a season. Present it to God as a prayer? Undoubtedly. But once that Word takes root deep within, we must begin to act upon it, an action that begins with our lips.

Let the Lord's miraculous Word sculpt your prayers. You cannot go wrong using the Word of God in your prayers when you apply it honestly and with compassion. My prayer for you is that you will come to understand the power of your voice, the authority of God's Word, and the satisfaction of the good fruit of your words" (Prov. 12:14). As you use WordSpeak, I pray God's Spirit will feed you richly from His banquet table and God's Word will become such a part of your being that it bursts with power from your lips. Blessings!

Your words were found and I ate them, and Your words became for me
a joy and the delight of my heart.

—Jeremiah 15:16

Section Three

Go!

Accepting Your Commission

Whom shall I send, and who will go for Us? Then I said,
"Here am I. Send me!"

—Isaiah 6:8

My Commitment

Let him who has My word speak My word in truth.

—Jeremiah 23:28

Today, _____ ,

I solemnly commit to:

Be diligent to present myself approved to God as a workman who does not need to be ashamed, accurately handling the word of truth (2 Tim. 2:15).

I will not use deception, nor distort the Word of God. On the contrary, I will set forth the truth plainly (2 Cor. 4:2).

I will cleanse myself and become a vessel for honor, sanctified, useful to the Master, prepared for every good work (2 Tim. 2:21).

I will have the same spirit of faith, according to what is written, "I believed, therefore I spoke" (2 Cor. 4:13), and I will speak God's Word to the world, the flesh, and the devil.

_____

Name

Chapter 30

The Story That Never Ends

Write it on a tablet for them, inscribe it on a scroll, that for the days to come it may be an everlasting witness.

—Isaiah 30:8

N ow it is your turn to record your stories of changed lives and circumstances. The account can be mundane or amazing. Let it include the joys and the sorrows. Use the lines of this chapter to begin the record of your prayer log, your partnership with Christ in doing His work on this earth. Remember, He longs to be gracious to you!

Date: _____

Prayer concern:

_____

_____

_____

_____

Scripture prayer:

_____

_____

_____

Answer:

_____

_____

_____

_____

Date: _____

Prayer concern:

_____

_____

_____

_____

Scripture prayer:

_____

_____

_____

Answer:

_____

_____

_____

_____

Date: _____

Prayer concern:

_____

_____

The Story That Never Ends

_____

_____

Scripture prayer:

_____

_____

_____

Answer:

_____

_____

_____

_____

Date: _____

Prayer concern:

_____

_____

_____

_____

Scripture prayer:

_____

_____

_____

Answer:

_____

_____

WordSpeak

_____

_____

Date: _____

Prayer concern:

_____

_____

_____

_____

Scripture prayer:

_____

_____

_____

Answer:

_____

_____

_____

_____

Product information:

The scripture cards and prayer products mentioned in this book can be purchased at our Web site, www.wordspeakonline.com. Click on the community tab to tell us of your testimonies or to ask for help. Purchase or download the CDs that accompany the book, and dive in to the process of transforming your mind and your life.

WinePressPublishing
Your Book, Defined.

To order additional copies of this book call:
1-877-421-READ (7323)
or please visit our Web site at
www.WinePressbooks.com

If you enjoyed this quality custom-published book,
drop by our Web site for more books and information.

www.winepressgroup.com
"Your partner in custom publishing."

LaVergne, TN USA
03 November 2010

203353LV00003B/4/P